A FIELD GUIDE to WHISKY

A FIELD GUIDE to
WHISKY

An EXPERT COMPENDIUM to TAKE YOUR PASSION and KNOWLEDGE to the NEXT LEVEL

HANS OFFRINGA

ARTISAN | NEW YORK

Library of Congress Cataloging-in-Publication Data

Names: Offringa, Hans, 1956– author.
Title: A field guide to whisky / Hans Offringa.
Description: New York : Artisan, [2017] | Includes index.
Identifiers: LCCN 2016038076 | ISBN 9781579657512
(hardback, paper over board)
Subjects: LCSH: Whiskey.
Classification: LCC TP605 .O39 2017 | DDC 663/.52—dc23
LC record available at https://lccn.loc.gov/2016038076

Design by Raphael Geroni

Artisan books are available at special discounts when purchased in bulk
for premiums and sales promotions as well as for fund-raising or educational
use. Special editions or book excerpts also can be created to specification.
For details, contact the Special Sales Director at the address below,
or send an e-mail to specialmarkets@workman.com.

For speaking engagements, contact speakersbureau@workman.com.

Published by Artisan
A division of Workman Publishing Co., Inc.
225 Varick Street
New York, NY 10014-4381
artisanbooks.com

Original Title: *Wat je als whiskyliefhebber moet weten*
Author: Hans Offringa
Research Manager: Becky Lovett Offringa
hansoffringa.com / thewhiskycouple.com
First published in the Netherlands in 2015 by Karakter Uitgevers B.V. in the series
Wat je als . . . moet weten.

Artisan is a registered trademark of Workman Publishing Co., Inc.

Published simultaneously in Canada by Thomas Allen & Son, Limited

Printed in China

3 5 7 9 10 8 6 4

To Duncan Elphick,
with gratitude

"CIVILIZATION BEGINS WITH DISTILLATION."

———————————————

William Faulkner

Contents

Introduction

Whisky is an alcoholic beverage that most likely originated in Ireland. Eventually the knowledge about distilling whisky spread to Scotland, which means that both countries are generally credited as the birthplace of the most complex drink in the world. Irish and Scottish distillers brought their knowledge with them when immigrating to the United States and Canada. In the first part of the twentieth-century, Japan more or less picked up the craft from Scotland. Today, whisky can be made anywhere in the world.

Whisky is made of grain, water, and yeast—but this is only the beginning of a long story. There are many different kinds of whisky, and although the basics are similar across the board, each country uses its own production methods. The same general principle applies: grains contain starch, which can be converted into fermentable sugars with the help of enzymes. When you dissolve those sugars in warm water, let the mixture cool for a while, and then add yeast, you get a liquid containing alcohol. The percentage of alcohol increases each time you heat the liquid up to a certain temperature. When the desired percentage is achieved, the distillate is poured into wooden casks and left to age until the end product is whisky ready for consumption. The minimum maturation times are different from country to country. By law, the ABV (alcohol by volume) percentage of the liquid must be at least 40 when the spirit is bottled as whisky.

Whisky has experienced a renaissance over the past decade and is growing in popularity among younger generations. Whether you are a complete novice interested in getting acquainted with the basics and learning how to pick a good-value bottle to get you started, or a whisky connoisseur looking for a great reference book, new developments, and current trends, *A Field Guide to Whisky* will become your favorite whisky companion. It will take you on a journey through the places where this diverse drink is being produced all over the world, from the famous "Big Five"—Scotland, Ireland, the United States, Canada, and Japan—to the

nooks and crannies you may least expect, like Tasmania, Taiwan, and South Africa. You'll learn about its history and the differences in how various kinds are produced; how to read a label; how to taste and discern complex flavor patterns to get the most out of your glass—even how to conduct a whisky master class during which you can share the experience with your friends. You'll find valuable tips on investing in whisky and learn about the diverse whisky scene in the United States and the rest of the world. Finally, numerous lists and maps of distilleries, whisky trails, hotels, festivals, bars, and clubs will provide invaluable information for getting out there and putting your newfound expertise to use—whether you choose to join a whisky society, visit a distillery, or discover a new whisky bar in your city.

CHAPTER 1

WHAT
IS
WHISKY?

1. What Are the Origins of the Word *Whisky*?

The word *whisky* is derived from the Gaelic *uisge beatha* (pronounced "ooshkie bayha"), also written as *usquebaugh*, which is derived from the Latin expression *aqua vita* (water of life). The English were not proficient in Gaelic and turned it into *uisgy*, which later morphed into *whisky* and *whiskey*.

2. Why Is Whisky Spelled With and Without an *E*?

In the past, both spellings were used interchangeably. Over time, the Irish and Americans chose *whiskey*, while the rest of the world, spearheaded by Scotland, chose *whisky*. But this is by no means a rule written in stone. For instance, Maker's Mark and Old Forester, both produced in the United States, write their names without the *e*, and a distillery in the Netherlands, Horstman, puts *whiskey* on its label. Throughout this book, *whisky* is used as the standard spelling, unless the entry is specifically about Irish or American whiskey.

3. What Are the Different Types of Whisky?

Whisky is divided into thirteen main categories:

1. Single malt whisky
2. Single grain whisky
3. Blended malt whisky
4. Blended grain whisky
5. Blended whisky
6. Bourbon whiskey
7. Tennessee whiskey
8. Rye whiskey
9. Wheat whiskey
10. Corn whiskey
11. Canadian whisky
12. Japanese whisky
13. Irish whiskey

Single malt whisky, single grain whisky, blended malt whisky, blended grain whisky, blended whisky, rye whiskey, wheat whiskey, and corn whiskey can be made anywhere in the world. Bourbon whiskey, Tennessee whiskey, Canadian whisky, Japanese whisky, and Irish whiskey are type-, country-, or region-specific. The country of origin has to be mentioned on the label, and more region-specific information is often added too, such as with whisky d'Alsace from France or whisky Español from Spain.

4. How Many Brands of Whisky Are There?

Thousands! A single distillery can produce multiple brands at once. This kind of production is more common among American and Irish distilleries than in Scotland and its worldwide counterparts. This is in part due to Prohibition, when many brand names from bankrupt and closed distilleries were bought by the surviving distilleries in their respective countries.

For example, the American distillery Heaven Hill produces more than a hundred different bourbons. Midleton Distillery in Cork, Ireland, produces at least seven well-known brands. Cooley Distillery in Dundalk, Ireland, is known for bringing pre-Prohibition Irish brands back to life for new customers. Blended Scotch can be tailor-made, in which case the customer gets to pick his or her own brand name. Another reason for using a different brand name is to distinguish one taste profile from another. For example, Springbank, in the south of Scotland, makes an eponymous single malt, alongside two different expressions named Longrow and Hazelburn. Tobermory on the Hebridean island of Mull distills an unpeated single malt called Tobermory and a peated expression named Ledaig.

5. Which Country Produces the Most Whisky?

It might not be the country that first comes to mind, but it is India that produces by far the most liters of whisky in the world. The annual list of the top thirty whisky producers announced by the whisky publication *Malt Whisky Yearbook* was topped in 2015 by Officer's Choice (214 million liters produced annually)—a whisky that is virtually unknown outside India. Johnnie Walker took second place with more than 180 million liters. This doesn't seem like such a huge difference, but there are seven more Indian blends in the top ten that, when combined with Officer's Choice, annually produce more than 1 billion liters! Jack Daniel's Tennessee Whiskey takes sixth place with 103.5 million liters.

The first bourbon on the list is Jim Beam (eleventh place) with 62 million liters. Canada debuts on the 2015 list at number thirteen with Crown Royal (49.5 million liters). Ireland's pride, Jameson, takes the seventeenth spot with 38.7 million liters. Japan's Kakubin is twenty-fifth on the list (25.2 million liters). The ten Scotch blends on the list account for 36.1 million liters combined, the best known among them being Chivas, Ballantine's, The Famous Grouse, and Dewar's. Then another five smaller Indian brands whose combined number is 18.2 million liters and an American blended whiskey, Seagram's 7 Crown, in thirtieth place with 21.6 million liters. Single malts—the grand crus among whiskies—do not show up on this list. Their largest producer, Glenfiddich, makes approximately 14 million liters annually.

Canada

Japan

Scotland

United States

Ireland

6. Which Countries Are the Biggest Exporters of Whisky?

Scotland, Ireland, the United States, Canada, and Japan are the key players on the world whisky scene. These countries are known as the Big Five because they produce the most well-known and widely distributed whiskies in the world.

India, by far the largest producer of blended whisky in the world, doesn't belong on this list because 90 percent of its production is consumed nationally. To boot, a significant portion of its whisky isn't made from grains but from sugar cane, so it cannot officially be considered whisky. However, India does make single malts on a small scale, Amrut and Paul John, and these brands have a presence in world export markets.

"TOO MUCH OF ANYTHING IS BAD,
BUT TOO MUCH GOOD WHISKEY IS
BARELY ENOUGH."

Mark Twain

7. What Does a Bottle of Whisky Cost?

A fine bottle of whisky can cost anywhere between $25 and $200. Scarce brands such as Pappy Van Winkle and limited-edition releases can even exceed $20,000 a bottle.

This is a big range because "fine" doesn't mean the same thing to everyone. Sometimes it would appear that there are shortages of certain bourbons and other whiskies, but these aren't so much shortages (more whisky is being produced today than ever before) as they are increases in demand for certain brands or expressions of whisky. This can mean that your favorite whisky is not always available at your local store due to allocation by producers and importers who are increasingly challenged with stock management. It can also mean that you'll pay more for the bottle when you do find it.

To make whisky, you have to have a long-term business plan, since the distillate has to mature for a certain period, usually years, before it can be sold as whisky. To complicate matters, it is hard to predict what people will drink in four to ten years. This has been a demanding business for centuries.

A good, easily attainable bottle of whisky can be found in a $20 to $70 price range (prices may differ by retailer).

8. Is Older Whisky Better Than Younger Whisky?

Older whiskies aren't necessarily better than younger ones per se. Age is a number; maturation is character. Some whiskies want to stay in the cask for a long time; others should be released into the world sooner. Producers also play around with different ages to increase the variety of their assortment while maintaining the quality of their products. If a whisky stays in the cask for too long, the product may become bitter and tannic. When a whisky has not matured long enough, the product usually is a bit raw and fiery, often out of balance.

9. Can Anybody Make Whisky?

The basic process of distillation is something you could do yourself, although making good whisky is far more difficult. But . . . playing with fire, methanol, and other volatile spirits can be extremely dangerous. More important, your government does not allow it—to start your own distillery, you have to collect numerous permits and licenses, and if you fail to do so, you are distilling illegally.

CHAPTER 2

WHISKY AROUND THE WORLD

10. Whisky Made in Scotland

Scotland produces five types of whisky:

1. **SINGLE MALT WHISKY** is made of malted barley and distilled in batches in copper pot stills. It is produced by one single distillery. The well-known brands include Glenfiddich, The Glenlivet, The Macallan, Lagavulin, Laphroaig, and Oban.

2. **SINGLE GRAIN WHISKY** is made of a different type of grain, usually corn or wheat, in thirty-foot-high column stills using a process of continuous distillation. Usually a small percentage of malted barley is added as a catalyst. The well-known brands include North British, Black Barrel, and Cameron Brig.

3. **BLENDED MALT WHISKY** is a mixture of single malts only, from various distilleries. There is no grain whisky in a blended malt. This type of whisky is sometimes called a vatted malt or a pure malt. The well-known brands include Odyssey, Monkey Shoulder, and Johnnie Walker Green Label.

4. **BLENDED GRAIN WHISKY** is a mixture of various grain whiskies. This is a rather rare type, not often seen on store shelves. Snow Grouse, the brother of The Famous Grouse, serves as a good example. Almost 90 percent of Scotch is blended whisky. By law in Scotland, all Scotch whisky has to mature in oak casks for a minimum of three years.

5. **BLENDED WHISKY** is a mixture of mature malt whiskies from various distilleries blended with a certain amount of mature grain whisky. The percentages of the two types vary by brand. The well-known brands include The Famous Grouse, Johnnie Walker, Ballantine's, Chivas Regal, Black Bottle, and Dewar's.

Eilean Donan Castle, a legendary landmark for whisky tourists on their way to
Talisker Distillery on the Isle of Skye.

11. Whiskey Made in Ireland

The Irish predominantly make blended whiskey and use pot stills as well as column stills. Some of the well-known examples are Jameson and Paddy. The Irish Republic produces single malts, such as Tyrconnell and Connemara. Single pot still whiskeys, which are a special type of whiskey native to Ireland, include Redbreast and Green Spot. This whiskey is distilled from a mixture of malted and unmalted barley, using a copper pot still. Grain whiskeys are rare, but there are exceptions like Kilbeggan, which is bottled as both a blend and a single grain whiskey.

Blends, grain whiskeys, and single pot still whiskeys are sometimes mixed to produce a unique expression, like Tullamore Dew.

Northern Ireland produces both blends, like Black Bush, and single malts, like Bushmills. In recent years, the number of distilleries in both Northern Ireland and the Republic of Ireland has grown from four to more than a dozen. The new kids on the block are mostly small craft distillers, such as Teeling Whiskey Co., which is in Dublin.

12. Whiskey Made in the United States

American whiskey is usually made of a mixture of different grains, following a specific recipe called a mash bill, and every distillery has its own version. The predominant grains are corn, rye, wheat, and malted barley. The five main types of whiskeys produced are as follows:

1. **BOURBON WHISKEY,** or bourbon for short, can be made anywhere in the United States, but the lion's share is produced in Kentucky. The main ingredient is corn. Well-known brands are Four Roses, Maker's Mark, Wild Turkey, and Jim Beam.

2. **TENNESSEE WHISKEY** can be made only in the eponymous state. This is the only region-specific whiskey made in the United States. Well-known brands are Jack Daniel's, George Dickel, and Prichard's.

3. **RYE WHISKEY,** mainly produced in Kentucky, has a substantial amount of rye at its core. Well-known brands include Old Overholt, Rittenhouse, George T. Stagg, and Sazerac.

4. **WHEAT WHISKEY** has a large proportion of wheat in its mash bill. This variety is rather rare. A good example is Bernheim.

5. **CORN WHISKEY** is made of at least 80 percent corn.

The United States also produces blended whiskey, which predominantly consists of neutral grain alcohol with small additions of bourbon or rye to flavor the drink. A well-known brand is Barton. Single malt whiskey (with an *e*), made from malted barley exclusively, is produced in small quantities by a few microdistillers producing for their local markets. The trend has spread like wildfire across the country in the last five years, with an abundance of new microdistilleries emerging as a result—a situation reminiscent of the sudden increase in the number of microbreweries a few decades ago. Some of these microdistilleries will flourish, but many will perish due to a lack of cash flow, liquid assets, or perceived quality.

13. **Whisky Made in Canada**

Canadian whisky is made in pot stills and column stills. The mash bill is a combination of corn, wheat, and rye, the latter being the most important part. Each ingredient is distilled and matured separately and then blended. Adding a small percentage (no more than 10 percent) of fruit wines to the whisky—which broadens the flavoring options—is allowed by law in Canada. Well-known brands include Canadian Club, Black Velvet, and Crown Royal.

Single malt whisky is made on a small scale by niche producers, and the product is sold in local markets only. As is the case in the United States, craft distilleries are increasing in number in Canada. Glen Breton from Nova Scotia is a good example.

14. **Whisky Made in Japan**

The Land of the Rising Sun follows the Scottish distilling traditions, with a few nuances of its own. Large quantities of Scotch were originally imported and blended with distillates native to Japan. In the last two and a half decades, single malts and blends produced entirely in Japan hit the worldwide market. They are known to be very aromatic. Well-known brands include Nikka, Yamazaki, Hakushu, and Hibiki.

Opposite: The slopes of Mount Fuji provide water for the Fuji-Gotemba Distillery.

15. Is Whisky Produced Anywhere Else in the World?

Whisky can be made anywhere in the world where grains can be grown and a supply of yeast and clean water is available. Since the late 1980s, sales of whisky have seen steady growth worldwide. Many small distilleries and breweries, often family-owned, decided to jump on the bandwagon and started producing a distillate from grains along with their usual production of schnapps, gin, fruit liqueurs, vodka, and brandy. Most Western European countries and Australasia have gone that route—even Taiwan has joined the whisky-making trend.

In the early 2000s throughout the United States, state governments began to relax their strict alcohol regulations—which often dated back to Prohibition—much to the benefit of small distillers. They made licensing more accessible and allowed the retail sale of alcoholic products on-site. Almost every state has one or more microdistilleries, with output generally limited to local sales. Not every micro- or craft distillery is producing whiskey; many are selling bulk whiskey bottled for their label. Kentucky and Tennessee are still by far the most important whiskey-producing states in the United States.

16. **Australian Whisky**

Australia has seen a true whisky revival in the past fifteen years. For more than a century, not a single drop of whisky was produced Down Under, but today Tasmania is a hotbed of craft distilleries, with names like Lark, Hellyers Road, Hobart, Bakery Hill, Nant, Sullivans Cove, and Overeem leading the way. The whiskies are mainly consumed within Australia, but they can sometimes be found in other parts of the world.

17. **Austrian Whisky**

John Heider, who started making whisky in 1995 in Roggenreith, is a pioneer among Austrian whisky distillers. Reisetbauer in Kirchberg started its production in 1995 as well. From 2002 to 2004, two more significant distilleries emerged, Destillerie Weutz and Old Raven. Today they are joined by thirteen other small liqueur and schnapps producers who also make a bit of whisky on the side.

18. **Belgian Whisky**

The Belgian Owl in Liège is the most popular whisky in the country. Then there is Goldlys, a whisky produced by Filliers, a gin manufacturer. Two other smaller distilleries are Radermacher and Gouden Carolus.

Belgian Single Malt Whisky

19. Czech Whisky

The Czechs have been players in the whisky world for some time, but their production is mainly for the domestic market. Gold Cock Distillery has been making whisky since 1877 and produces two different expressions. They are rarely found outside the country, but they do show up at Maltstock (see Resources, page 303) once in a while.

20. Danish Whisky

Braunstein in Copenhagen, Fary Lochan in Give, and Stauning in Skjern are the three crown jewels of Danish whisky. Recently, alcohol industry giant Diageo invested £10 million (about $13 million) in Stauning, which shows that the Vikings are expected to become important competitors on the world scene in the years to come. Braunstein, a company that grew out of a brewery, is slowly conquering export markets.

"THERE IS NO BAD WHISKEY. THERE ARE ONLY SOME WHISKEYS THAT AREN'T AS GOOD AS OTHERS."

Raymond Chandler

21. Dutch Whisky

The Netherlands has two commercial distilleries. The first one is the brewer Us Heit (Frisian for "our father"), which is located in the old northern town of Bolsward. Since 2004, it has been producing a single malt called Frysk Hynder ("the Frisian thoroughbred"). The second one is Zuidam Distillers in Baarle-Nassau, a southern Dutch enclave surrounded by Belgium. Zuidam started in the 1970s as a jenever (gin) distiller and soon branched out into fruit liqueurs and vodka. In 1999, the company began distilling whisky and currently produces single malts and rye whisky under the brand name Millstone. There are also a number of microdistillers spread around the country. The following are worth a mention: Kalkwijck Distillers—with the only female owner and master distiller in Western Europe (and maybe even the world)—Erve Sculte, Kampen Distillers, IJsvogel, and Pronckheur.

22. English Whisky

When Alfred Barnard published his magnum opus, *The Whisky Distilleries of the United Kingdom*, in 1887, he mentioned ten active distilleries, of which only four were worth an entry: Vauxhall and Bank Hall in Liverpool, Bristol in Bristol, and Lea Valley in London. They were closed down a long time ago, and England had been getting by without a single whisky distillery for more than a century. This changed in 2006, when the Nelstrop family founded

St George's Distillery in Norfolk. In recent years, a few others have joined the ranks: Adnams in Southwold, the London Distillery Company, the Lakes Distillery in Cumbria, and Hicks & Healey in Cornwall.

23. Finnish Whisky

The Finns started making whisky in the 1950s, but it wasn't until the 1980s that any of their product was bottled as such. Not terribly successful, the operation was closed in 1995. Seven years later, Teerenpeli was born out of a brewery located in Yhtiöt Oy. In 2014, Kyrö in Isokyrö joined the ranks.

24. French Whisky

The oldest and most well-known whisky distillery in France is Glann Ar Mor in Bretagne, founded in 1999 by Jean Donnay. Jean and his wife are currently in the process of building the Gartbreck Distillery on the Scottish island of Islay. Other French whisky distillers are Warenghem in Lannion, Des Menhirs in Plomelin, Meyer in Hohwarth, Elsass in Obernai, Domaine des Hautes Glaces in Rhône-Alpes, Guillon in La Champagne, and Brenne in the Cognac region.

25. German Whisky

Germany has an abundance of small craft distilleries, each of them producing fruit and grain distillates. The oldest one among them is Schraml in Erbendorf, founded in 1818. Since whisky has grown in popularity, even the smallest distilleries strive toward finding their place on the market. Almost all whisky distilled in Germany is consumed locally. Notable brands include Blaue Maus from Eggolsheim, Slyrs from Schliersee, Finch from Nellingen, and Liebl from Bad Kötzting.

Above: Slyrs Distillery in Schliersee, Germany. *Opposite:* Puni Distillery in Glorenza, Italy.

26. Icelandic Whisky

It's only in the past two decades that temperatures in Iceland have been mild enough to allow for the successful growth of barley. On the other hand, potatoes have always been abundant and used for distilling, though the product of those distillations isn't whisky. So thanks to climate change, since 2009 Iceland has been producing its own authentic whisky, called Flóki.

27. Italian Whisky

For decades, Italy has been importing large quantities of malt whisky from Scotland. The Italians' love for Scottish whisky is perfectly demonstrated by the fact that Campari, an Italian beverage company, owns Glen Grant—a very popular Scottish single malt made in Rothes, Speyside. Since 2010, the Italians have made their own whisky at Puni—a distillery located in Southern Tirol that stands out because of its striking cube-like shape.

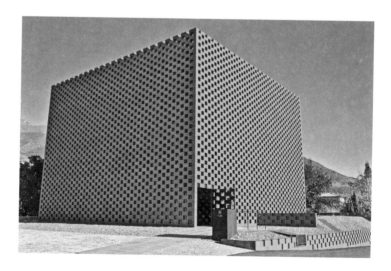

28. Norwegian Whisky

For many years, distilling was under a state monopoly in Norway. This changed in 2009 with the privatization of Arcus, a large producer of aquavit and vodka. Their distillery in Hagan immediately branched out and now produces Gjoleid whisky in various expressions.

29. South African Whisky

James Sedgwick of the Distell Group—which owns Scottish distilleries Tobermory, Deanston, and Bunnahabhain—has been producing two types of whisky in Wellington for many years: a grain whisky called Bain's and a ten-year-old single malt called Three Ships. It's a Goliath next to the much smaller Drayman's in Pretoria, which produces the Drayman's Highveld whisky. Its owner, Moritz Kallmeyer, started a beer pub annex brewery in 1990 and later specialized in making whisky as well.

30. **South American Whisky**

The inhabitants of the South American continent have been consuming Scotch whisky for more than a hundred years. Since 2008, Union Distillery in Veranópolis, Brazil, has been producing a single malt called Union Club; and in 2011, a single malt distillery called La Alazana was founded in Los Golondrinas, Argentina.

31. **Spanish Whisky**

Spain has had a long relationship with Scotch whisky. In particular, the single malt Cardhu enjoyed a large following among Spanish consumers who drank it mixed with Coke. However, in recent years its popularity has declined. Today, Spain has two of its own distilleries that make whisky. The larger one is Destilerías y Crianza (DYC), founded in 1963. The other is Embrujo, which is somewhat older and much smaller. Spanish whiskies are rarely encountered outside the Iberian Peninsula.

32. Swedish Whisky

The Swedes are considered "mature consumers" by the international whisky industry. A new variety of whisky regularly debuts in Sweden before being introduced into other markets. This was the case a few years ago with The Black Grouse, peaty brother of The Famous Grouse. But the Swedes distill their own whisky too. Mackmyra started in 1999 in Gävle and can now be found in many countries in Western Europe. Others followed, such as the very promising Box from Bjärtrå, Smögen from Hunnebostrand, and Spirit of Hven from the tiny island of Hven off of Sweden's southern coast.

Box Distillery, situated in the northeast of Sweden.

33. Swiss Whisky

It wasn't until 1999 that the Swiss government lifted a ban on distilling whisky. Locher in Appenzell has been successful with its Säntis Malt for several years. Two other significant producers are Langatun in Langenthal and Whisky Castle in Elfingen, both founded in 2002. With that law change, Switzerland witnessed an explosion of microdistilleries producing small quantities for local consumption similar to that of Austria and Germany.

34. Taiwanese Whisky

Although China isn't making whisky (yet!), Taiwan has been for some time. In 2006, the renowned Scottish firm Forsyth's built King Car Kavalan Whisky Distillery in Yilan. Its whiskies—King Car, Solist, and Kavalan—are beginning to make a name for themselves in world markets and have already won various prizes in international competitions.

King Car Kavalan Distillery in Taiwan.

35. Turkish Whisky

Tekel (Turkish for "monopoly") is this country's only distillery and is fully controlled by the government. True to its name, this is the only whisky legally manufactured in Turkey and is sold only in the country itself.

36. Welsh Whisky

There is no mention of any Welsh distilleries in Alfred Barnard's *Whisky Distilleries of the United Kingdom*. Penderyn, a distillery situated in the beautiful surroundings of Brecon Beacons National Park, was founded in 2000 and claims to have revived the art of distillation a hundred years after it had disappeared from Wales. Its single malts, the majority of which have been extra-matured in former Madeira casks, are sold worldwide.

37. Does Whisky Have an Appellation Like Wine Does?

Appellation (*contrôlée*) is the legally defined and protected geographical designation used, especially in France, to ascertain where the grapes for a wine were grown. The system is based on precisely defined wine regions. For example, champagne can be called champagne only when its grapes and the final product come from that specific region. Otherwise the beverage is considered sparkling wine.

In the whisky world, it is common practice to state the region of origin. That's where the whisky has to be made, matured, and, in most cases, bottled. However, the grains used may come from a different region, state, or even country.

The label on a Scottish single malt whisky often shows the region of origin. The Scotch Whisky Association (SWA) uses the following division: Highlands, Speyside, Islay, Lowlands, and Campbeltown. Various whisky writers also include Islands as one of the regions.

In earlier days, the region was solely an indicator of the taste of the whisky, but nowadays it primarily serves as an indication of the geographical area where the whisky is produced.

The label can say Scotch only when the whisky has been distilled, matured, bottled, and blended in Scotland.

Along the same lines, bourbon can be called bourbon only when it's distilled in the United States. Jack Daniel's distinguishes itself with the moniker Tennessee whiskey, as do George Dickel and Prichard's, located in the same state.

Whisky can be called Irish whiskey only if it was produced in Ireland, and Canadian whisky only if it was distilled in Canada. Japanese whisky, on the other hand, can be either 100 percent Japanese or a blend of Japanese and Scotch whiskies. For the rest of the world, a rule of thumb applies: if the label contains the name of a country, the whisky in the bottle has to be produced in said country.

38. **Whisky and Terroir**

In the wine industry, the word *terroir* is commonly used to describe the entire natural environment in which a specific grape is grown, whereas in the whisky industry, the concept is rarely used. For whisky, it is much more important where the production took place, because the microclimate in situ has an influence on the maturation process. Scotch whisky, for example, doesn't have to be distilled from grain grown in Scotland. The market price is usually a deciding factor when sourcing the grain. Much of the barley used in Scotch whisky comes from England and even from Canada and Australia. However, a few distilleries do produce whisky that is partly made of barley grown on their own estates, such as The Macallan and Bruichladdich in Scotland and Eastmoor in the Netherlands.

Opposite: Barley fields near Rothes in the Speyside region of Scotland.

CHAPTER 3

FROM GRAIN TO GLASS

MALT WHISKY

Stages of Malt Whisky Production

1. Harvesting

2. Malting

3. Kilning

4. Milling

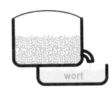

5. Mashing

6. Fermenting

7. Distilling

8. Maturing

9. Bottling

10. Drinking

Find out more about each production stage in the following entries:

Stages 1–8: entries 39–116

Stage 9: entries 191–220

Stage 10: entries 222–50

39. How Is Malt Whisky Made?

Water, barley, yeast, and energy are the four things needed to make malt whisky. That sounds simple. But the process itself is much more complicated and can be further divided into the following steps: malting, kilning, milling, mashing, fermenting, distilling, maturing, and bottling.

40. Where Does the Water Come From?

Water is used at every step in the process of making whisky—and lots of it. This is one of the main reasons why most distilleries are located in the vicinity of a significant water source like a river or a spring and usually own their own springs. The water drawn from a spring and used for the actual whisky making is called "process water." The water used in the condensers does not come into direct contact with the distillate and is called "cooling water." It is normally drawn from a river nearby but can also be taken from the nearest municipality's drinking-water source.

41. Does the Type of Water Used Affect the Whisky?

Water has an important influence on the whisky produced. It starts with the source and the condition of the soil. Water that streams over relatively soft soil, such as sand or limestone, absorbs more minerals than water flowing over hard, rocky terrain. Each type of soil contains different minerals. For example, the granite soil found in parts of Scotland's Speyside is very hard and doesn't contain many minerals, resulting in water that is pure and soft. In the Northern Highlands around Tain, though, the water is hard because it rises up to the surface through limestone, which is a sedimentary rock largely composed of calcium carbonate. On the Isle of Islay, the water flows over peaty soil, which contains decayed seaweed and sphagnum (a type of moss) that release phenols. Phenols are the compounds responsible for the smoky taste of some whiskies (see entries 46 and 47). However, it is unlikely that phenols in water are noticeable in the final whisky. The mineral content of water only influences the fermentation stage. When bottled, whisky is diluted with demineralized water, which doesn't affect the flavor of the end product.

42. **What Types of Grains Are Used?**

Barley is the grain with the most flavor, and improving barley strains is a continuous effort, both for the farmer and the distiller. The former is interested in as large a harvest per square meter as possible; the latter in the highest possible yield of alcohol from a ton of barley. Cultivating new varieties is an ongoing process, especially because barley is very vulnerable to fungi—even strains that were previously resistant. Well-known barley strains are Golden Promise, Minstrel, Concerto, and Optimum.

"THERE ARE TWO THINGS
A HIGHLANDER LIKES NAKED,
AND THE OTHER ONE IS
MALT WHISKY."

Sir Robert Bruce Lockhart

43. Where Does the Barley Come From?

The general consensus is that the type of barley and its pedigree hardly influence the end product. Scotch, after all, doesn't have to be distilled from Scottish barley. The majority of the barley used for Scotch is imported from England, Canada, Europe, or Australia. Price is usually the main factor when deciding where to get the grain. However, the suppliers have to follow the distilleries' specifications to a T when delivering

the barley, which can be as specific as the expected yield of alcohol per ton of barley. Some distilleries, like Bruichladdich, Benromach, and The Macallan, are particular about the pedigree of their barley and source it locally. The barley has to be malted before it can be used, which takes about a week. During this time, barley, now called "green malt," becomes saturated with natural sugars, which will produce alcohol later in the distillation process.

Barley may be sourced anywhere; it is not necessarily from the country where the whisky is distilled.

44. What Is Malting?

Before it can be used, barley has to be malted—steeped in large steel water vessels for two to three days. During this time the grain becomes soft and sticky and starts to germinate. Small sprouts grow from the kernels, enzymes are released, and the starch in the grain is converted into maltose (a kind of sugar). Next, the grains are spread out on the malting floor to germinate; they're turned regularly to prevent overheating. A handful of distilleries still turn the germinating malt manually by using a wooden spade (shiel) or a motorized device resembling a small lawn mower. Germination takes about a week, during which the "green malt" becomes saturated with natural sugars that will produce alcohol during distillation. Because this traditional process is quite labor intensive, nowadays it is largely mechanized and centralized. The majority of the barley comes from large commercial malting plants in Scotland that use centrifuges for the malting process.

Germinating barley on the edge of a steeping tank—the vessel used to soak the barley prior to spreading it on the malting floor.

45. What Is Kilning?

To stop germination, the barley needs to be dried. That happens in a drying oven, or kiln, using hot air. The chimney of many Scottish kilns has a pagoda-shaped fan, an innovation of architect Charles Doig in the nineteenth century. Now most distilleries buy their malted barley from large commercial maltings that produce their malt according to precise specifications. However, the pagodas on former kilns can be seen throughout Scotland.

Left: The industrial drum malting plant at Port Ellen on Islay. *Right:* At Bowmore, the turning of the malt is still partly done by hand.

46. How Does Peat Smoke Affect the Malted Barley?

When peat is used to fuel the fire in the kiln, the whisky will have a distinctive smoky flavor. A distiller can specify the exact peat level to be used while drying, to make sure his whisky flavor is consistent. One can purchase stocks of malted barley with varying peat levels, which allow the distiller to produce different expressions from the same stills, ranging from a non-peated to a heavily peated whisky. So the smoky note in a whisky doesn't come from water that contains peat but from burning peat in the kiln during the malting process.

Left: The old kiln of Aberfeldy, with its distinctive pagoda-shaped chimney.
Right: A peat fire in the kiln at Highland Park, Orkney.

47. **What Are Phenols?**

The desired peat level is noted in the malt specification, expressed in parts per million (ppm) phenol. Phenols are organic compounds found in peat smoke and in barley. They are aromatic substances similar to alcohol. Phenol used to be called carbolic acid. There are nine different phenols in peat smoke, each carrying a specific aroma. The source of the peat is important too. For example, Highland Park (from the Orkneys in Scotland) has a distinctly different peaty character than Lagavulin (made on the Isle of Islay).

48. **Why Is the Malted Barley Milled?**

Once at the distillery, the malt is strained through a large sieve to remove stones or debris and then transported to a mill that grinds it into a coarse flour called grist. This is essential for the next step: mashing.

The malt mill at Tobermory, Isle of Mull.

49. **What Is Mashing?**

Mashing is mixing grist with warm water in a huge vessel called the mash tun. This results in a thick "porridge" that is stirred constantly by a giant mechanical mixer. The maltose in the grist dissolves in the water and the remaining sweet liquid, called wort, is drained out of the mash tun. After cooling, the wort is ready for fermentation.

Mash tuns are usually closed vessels, like this one at Ardmore.

50. What Is a Mash Tun?

A mash tun is a brewing vessel made of cast iron or stainless steel wherein the grist is mixed with warm water. The bottom is a sieve that can be opened and closed. Once it is opened, the liquid can flow into the underback, while the solids stay in the mash tun (see entry 53).

51. What Is an Underback?

The container that catches the wort when the sieve in the mash tun is opened is called the underback. It catches the liquid before it is pumped to a washback (see entry 54).

52. What Is the Influence of Water During Mashing?

Mashing takes lots of water. It is done in two or three cycles, depending on the preferences of the distiller; the water temperature may differ at each cycle. The quality of the water and the substances found in it are very important during this phase. Too many minerals, like copper or iron, could cause problems during fermentation, which is the next step in the process. The acidity of the water is also important and affects the forming of esters (chemical compounds) during fermentation.

53. **What Is Draff?**

Draff is the residue left in the mash tun; it's later used as cattle feed. Distilling whisky is, in a way, based on the cradle-to-cradle principle: the draff returns to the food chain, serving as food for cows, and their manure enriches the soil where barley is grown.

54. **What Is a Washback?**

A washback is a fermentation vessel made of wood or stainless steel. All washbacks used to be made of wood—predominantly Oregon pine, Douglas fir, or Siberian larch—which required them to be replaced after fifty to sixty years of daily use. Many distilleries have switched to stainless steel because it's more economical, requires less maintenance, and is easier to clean.

MASH TUN

In Deanston's open mash tun, the mixer stirring the mash is clearly visible.

55. Stainless Steel Versus Wooden Washbacks

Those distillers that made the switch from wooden washbacks to stainless steel ones will mostly claim that it does not affect the taste of the whisky. Those who still use traditional wooden washbacks emphasize that it does. Washbacks are cleaned after each cycle with high-pressure steam and hot water, and there is a realistic chance that some microorganisms are left on the wooden washbacks. This surely adds to the taste of the end product.

Left: Wooden washbacks at Glenrothes. *Right:* Stainless steel washbacks at Tomatin.

56. What Is Fermentation?

Fermentation, occasionally referred to as yeasting, is nothing more than changing the chemical structure of a liquid with the use of micro-organisms. Yeast is a single-cell fungus that feeds on oxygen and multiplies at a fast rate. This is called aerobic fermentation. Yeast is also capable of converting sugars into alcohol and carbon dioxide, which is called anaerobic fermentation. The anaerobic reaction between yeast and glucose is expressed with the following formula: $C_6H_{12}O_6$ (glucose) $\rightarrow$ $2C_2H_5OH$ (ethanol) $+ 2CO_2$. This is the fermentation process that makes whisky. When yeast is added to the wort in the washback, the liquid starts foaming and frothing aggressively and sugars are converted into carbon dioxide and alcohol. A chemical reaction is set off with the acids in the malt, which creates esters and aldehydes. We perceive them as different aromas of fruits and flowers.

Foaming wash in a washback at Aberfeldy.

57. How Does the Yeast Influence the Flavor?

Yeast itself does not contribute any flavors or aromas to the finished product. Flavor is created during fermentation. The aromas we associate with flowers and fruit come from a combination of many different esters. For example, n-pentyl acetate has a distinctive aroma of bananas.

58. What Kinds of Yeast Are Used in Fermentation?

Early on, fermentation used to be spontaneous, when free-roaming fungi in nature and on people, animals, and plants could trigger the process. However, dedicated yeast strains were developed for bakers, brewers, and distillers over time. At first, all three types were used in the whisky industry, but gradually the switch was made to only distiller's yeast, which can be used in solid or liquid form. The most commonly used distiller's yeast brands are Mauri, Quest, and Kerry. Some craft distillers may still use brewer's yeast or baker's yeast.

59. **Where Do the Distilleries Get Their Yeast?**

Most world distilleries buy their yeast from a specialized production plant, with the exception of American distilleries, where yeast strains are usually kept alive on the distillery grounds. It is not uncommon for an American distiller to use various yeast strains to make one whiskey. Four Roses straight bourbon is a good example—no less than five yeast strains are used in its production. However, most distilleries worldwide use one yeast strain.

60. **How Long Does Fermentation Take?**

The fermentation process differs from distillery to distillery. A minimum of forty-eight hours is a regular cycle, but sixty to seventy hours is not uncommon. A few distillers will even allow a hundred-hour fermentation cycle. The length of fermentation affects the flavors and aromas of the drink, as more esters develop over time. However, allowing fermentation to go on for too long may cause bacteria to form, which can lead to undesired flavors and aromas like butyric acid. The remaining liquid at the end of fermentation is called "wash."

61. What Is the Wash?

The wash is a product of fermentation in a washback. It is a liquid resembling heavy beer, with an ABV (see entry 204) of between 7 and 9 percent, which gets pumped into a pot still ready for distilling.

62. What Is a Wash Still?

A wash still, used during the first round of distillation, gets filled with the wash from the washback and heated. A window on the neck of the still allows the distiller to monitor how rapidly the still is heated. The distillate coming from the wash still is called "low wines."

63. What Is a Pot Still?

A pot still is a hefty copper kettle used to distill the wash. Historically, each distillery has its own still shapes, and the shape influences the flavor. There are three basic shapes of pot stills: the onion, the lantern, and the pear.

Right: An onion-shaped pot still at Bowmore Distillery. *Opposite:* A lantern-shaped pot still at Jura Distillery; a pear-shaped pot still at Lagavulin Distillery.

64. How Does a Pot Still Work?

The still with the wash—alcoholic liquid resembling beer—is heated directly or indirectly. The boiling point of alcohol is lower than that of water, and the alcohol fumes rise up the neck of the still and enter a condenser (either a worm tub or a shell and tube; see page 69). The fumes condense into an oily fluid containing approximately 22 percent ABV. This liquid is pumped to a second, smaller vessel, called the spirit still, where the process is repeated a second time while the condensed alcoholic liquid is separated into foreshots (heads), middle cut, and feints (tails). Only the liquid from the middle cut is suitable for making whisky.

65. **What Is a Spirit Still?**

A spirit still is used during the second round of distillation, in which the ABV is increased again. It is filled with the distillate (low wines) from the wash still. When heated and condensed, the liquid passes through a spirit safe, where foreshots, middle cut, and feints are separated.

66. **What Is a Purifier?**

A purifier is connected to the still to promote reflux (see entry 70).

67. **What Is a Lyne Arm?**

The lyne arm, sometimes called a lye pipe, is the part of the still that connects the neck with the condenser. The angle at which it is connected, which can vary from a perfect 90 degrees to ascending or descending, will influence the distillate.

68. **What Is a Swan Neck?**

The swan neck connects the base of the still to the lyne arm, and the longer it is, the lighter the distillate will be. The stills at Glenmorangie, for example, have extremely long necks and are nicknamed "the giraffes" in the industry. In contrast, The Macallan has small, squat stills with short necks, resulting in a heavier distillate with a similar body. This is no indication of the qualities of these whiskies but points to a certain style.

69. **What Is a Boil Ball?**

A boil ball is a round widening between the base of the still and its neck. It promotes reflux (see entry 70).

Parts of the still: 1. purifier; 2. lyne arm; 3. swan neck; 4. boil ball.

70. **What Is Reflux?**

Reflux is a process whereby certain alcohol fumes condense in the still before reaching the condenser. They return to liquid form, fall back into the still, and are redistilled. Reflux promotes a delicate distillate.

71. **Why Do Pot Still Shapes Differ?**

Over time, each distillery has established its own preference regarding still shape based on the type and amount of spirit it produces. When a still has to be replaced, the coppersmith will create a new one with the exact same shape. A change in shape means a change in flavor.

72. **Why Are Pot Stills Made of Copper?**

Copper has a few important characteristics. First of all, it is easy to mold into a desired shape. Second, copper acts as a catalyst in the process and removes undesired elements, like sulfur compounds, from the distillate. Third, copper is an excellent heat conductor.

Scale models of Glenmorangie's and The Macallan's pot stills.

73. What Is a Condenser?

A condenser cools the alcohol fumes that rise from the still. There are two different types in use today. The first one is called a worm tub, a large vessel made of wood or steel, with a copper spiral tube immersed in cold water. The fumes travel down through the spiral and condense into liquid. The worm tub is an older piece of equipment—many distilleries have switched to the other type, the shell and tube condenser, which works the opposite way. The fumes rise through a column where small copper pipes are filled with cold water. Both condensers perform the same job, but the type of condensation does influence the body and taste of the eventual whisky.

Old-fashioned worm tub condensers at Talisker, on the Isle of Skye.

Top: Shell and tube condensers at Tobermory, on the Isle of Mull. *Above:* The spirit safe at Bowmore.

74. What Is Direct Heating?

Most pot stills used to be heated over an open fire. However, health-and-safety regulations banned open fires, and a switch has been made to external heating below the still. This is called direct heating. If caramelization occurs on the bottom of the still, which sometimes happens, the residue is removed by a rummager.

75. What Is a Rummager?

A rummager is a chain used for scraping away the residue on the bottom of the still.

76. What Is Indirect Heating?

Pot stills can also be heated indirectly, by means of steam coils or steam pans placed inside the lower part of the still. This type of heating prevents caramelization and, more important, makes it easier to monitor and regulate the distilling temperature.

77. What Is a Spirit Safe?

The spirit safe separates the foreshots, middle cut, and feints (see entries 78–80) during the second round of distillation. In some distilleries this process is automated, in others it is still done by hand. The distiller is most interested in the middle cut, which will be used for maturation. Using a thermometer and a hydrometer, he measures the temperature and relative density of the distillate and decides when to turn the handle.

78. What Are Foreshots?

Foreshots are highly volatile alcohols, some of which are not suitable for consumption, like methanol. They are separated during the second round of distillation in the spirit safe and redistilled in a subsequent round.

79. What Is the Middle Cut?

The middle cut, a liquid containing somewhere between 60 and 70 percent ABV, is also referred to as "the heart of the run." It is transferred into a vessel called the spirit receiver, and the liquid is pumped to the filling store, where it is poured into oak casks.

80. What Are Feints?

Feints are heavy alcohols and fusel oils. Some may negatively influence the taste of the eventual whisky. Therefore, they are separated and redistilled in a subsequent round in the spirit still.

81. What Is a Feints Receiver?

This is a large container that catches the feints (tails or aftershots) before they are redistilled with the next batch.

82. What Is a Low Wines Receiver?

A low wines receiver is a container that collects the distillate from the wash still before it's pumped into the spirit still.

83. **What Is New Make Spirit?**

New make spirit is the newly distilled spirit ready for maturation in casks. It is a colorless liquid containing between 63.5 and 70 percent ABV. An old-fashioned name for it is "clearic."

84. **What Is a Spirit Receiver?**

The spirit receiver is the vessel that contains the new make spirit before it is pumped to the filling store.

85. **What Is Pot Ale?**

The residue in the wash still after distillation is called the pot ale. It is rich in proteins and used for feeding cattle, as fertilizer, and as fuel to generate energy.

86. **What Are Spent Lees?**

The residue in the spirit still after distillation is called the spent lees. It will be filtered in an effluent plant and discarded, usually in a nearby river, since it can't be used further.

87. **What Is Triple Distillation?**

The majority of malt whiskies are distilled twice, with the exception of a few, like Auchentoshan. This Lowlander is typically distilled three times, consecutively in a wash still, an intermediate still, and a spirit still. The result is a softer, gentler distillate. Hazelburn from Springbank in Campbeltown is also a triple-distilled single malt. In Ireland, triple distillation is more widespread.

The trio of pot stills at Auchentoshan, located west of the city of Glasgow.

88. How Does Spirit Get into a Cask?

The filling of the casks (or barrels) happens in the filling store. Most malt whisky is diluted with demineralized water to 63.5 percent ABV before it goes into the cask.

89. How Long Does Whisky Mature?

Scotch, by law, has to mature a minimum of three years in a bonded warehouse. The liquid cannot be considered whisky until the three-year mark and is instead called *new make spirit* or simply *spirit* until then. Many other countries follow the three-year rule, regardless of whether it is imposed by law. In the United States and Canada, different rules apply.

90. What Is a Dunnage Warehouse?

An old traditional warehouse that is usually one or two stories tall, with thick stone walls and an earthen floor, is called a dunnage warehouse. Each floor can hold up to three stacked casks of spirit. Only a few distilleries continue to use this type of warehouse, the main reason being that it is less efficient in terms of storage and space. Some beautiful examples of this style of storage can be seen at Glenfarclas in Speyside and Balblair in the Northern Highlands.

Top: Casks with maturing whisky in the dunnage warehouses at Balblair.
Above: Balblair Distillery.

91. **What Is a Racked Warehouse?**

This modern type of warehouse contains huge racks where casks can be stacked fifteen to twenty high per row. Often the casks are palletized in an upright position, which helps the warehouse workers easily move them. The majority of distilleries have stopped maturing their whisky in the traditional dunnage warehouses at the distillery. Instead the casks are transported to a racked warehouse in the vicinity of a central bottling plant. Most whisky in Scotland is stored in huge warehouses in the "belt" between Edinburgh and Glasgow.

Left: In racked warehouses, casks are stacked horizontally in racks.
Right: Casks are palletized and stored vertically as well, predominantly in Ireland.

92. Does Whisky Always Mature in Wooden Casks?

Whisky has to mature in wooden casks, otherwise the bottled spirit isn't whisky. Most countries specify oak as the only permitted wood for casks. The character of the wood has a huge influence on the eventual taste of the whisky.

93. What Types of Oak Are Used?

The Scottish whisky industry predominantly uses American and European oak, specifically the *Quercus alba* (white oak), *Quercus robur* (summer oak), and *Quercus petraea* (winter oak) species. In recent years, other species have been experimented with. Japan, for example, matures part of its whisky in casks built from the indigenous mizunara oak tree (*Quercus mongolica*).

94. What Is a Barrel?

A barrel is an alcohol-storing container made of American white oak and has a maximum volume of 200 liters (53 gallons). Almost all American whiskey matures in this type of vessel. Barrels may also be used by sherry bodegas to prepare them for a second act—use in the Scottish malt whisky industry.

95. How Is a Barrel Made?

An oak has to grow between eighty and ninety years before it is suitable to be used as material for barrels. The trees are specially selected and felled. After having lain in the open air for six months, they are put in a drying oven until the humidity in the wood is reduced to 12 percent. The tree is then split in two, and each part is sawed in half again to get four pieces. From each piece, four staves are sawed in such a way that the orientation of the growth rings reduces the risk of a leaky barrel. The planks, approximately thirty-eight inches long, are delivered to a cooperage and cut into staves of the desired length, as well as heads and ends. Both barrel ends are toasted lightly in a special oven. A new barrel is made ("raised") using twenty-nine to thirty-one staves, held together by a temporary ring. It will then be steam heated to make the wood more pliable. The barrel is tightened with a winch and fitted with temporary hoops that come from a large roll of flexible iron bands. Then it's ready to be toasted and charred from the inside. When charring is done, the barrel is lightly scraped and the head and end are fitted, after which the barrel has to cool off. The temporary hoops are removed, and when the barrel is cooled enough, the permanent hoops—usually six in total—are placed on it. The cooper bores the bung-hole in the widest stave. A gallon of water is poured into the barrel, after which it is sealed with a rubber stop and pressurized to check for leakages. At the end of the production line, each barrel is inspected for quality and any existing leaks are repaired.

There are three large cooperages in the United States and two in Scotland. Some distilleries, mainly in Scotland and Ireland, have on-site cooperages.

"Raising a barrel" at the Bluegrass Cooperage, Louisville, Kentucky.

96. Why Are New Barrels Charred or Toasted?

Toasting or charring a barrel "opens" the wood up so that the whisky stored inside can physically and chemically interact with it. Experts estimate that at least 60 percent of the aroma and taste of a whisky comes from the wood's influence.

97. What Are the Main Characteristics of American Oak?

American oak carries sweeter notes, such as vanilla, citrus, and coconut, but also spicier ones such as nutmeg and cloves. It may also give off less color, especially when used a second or third time, but this isn't always the case.

98. What Are the Main Characteristics of European Oak?

European oak usually carries darker notes, such as dried fruit and toffee. It may give the whisky a more intense color.

99. What Types of Barrels Are Used?

The whisky world has never been too picky regarding the type of barrel. The Scots have a preference for barrels (or casks, as they call them) that previously contained bourbon, sherry, port, rum, or wine. Each of these types of cask has a different name, as described in the following entries.

100. **What Is a Butt?**

A butt is a cask that holds between 500 and 600 liters; it is usually used for maturing sherry.

101. **What Is a Puncheon?**

A puncheon has the same volume as a butt, but it has a somewhat shorter and thicker shape. Puncheons are usually used for maturing sherry before being used to mature whisky.

102. **What Is a Hogshead?**

A hogshead is a vessel slightly larger than a barrel; it can hold up to 250 liters of liquid. Hogsheads are delivered ready-made from a cooperage but can also be made from a barrel by extending it with a few extra staves and replacing the head and the end. They can be used for maturing sherry prior to maturing whisky.

103. **What Is a Port Pipe?**

A port pipe is a type of cask used to mature port. Some malt distillers love to treat their whisky with an extra maturation in a port pipe after it has spent years in a former bourbon barrel. Finishing whisky in a separate barrel (see entry 115) adds extra nuances in flavor and aroma. Balvenie Portwood and Glenmorangie Quinta Ruban are fine examples of portwood finished single malts.

104. **What Is a Quarter Cask?**

A quarter cask is no longer considered a standard size. Originally, a quarter cask was a quarter of a sherry butt, holding 150 liters; however, quarter casks of 180 liters are no exception today. Quarter casks are used to speed up maturation, having a greater surface-to-volume ratio than larger cask types. The smaller the cask, the greater the wood influence on the spirit. Laphroaig has named one of its expressions Quarter Cask—a single malt that spent some time maturing in 125-liter casks. Quarter casks are the same height as bourbon barrels but more slender.

105. **What Is Virgin Oak?**

Virgin oak is a brand-new oak cask that hasn't previously held any liquid. Various single malts are currently being matured in such casks, prime examples being Deanston Virgin Oak and Glen Garioch Virgin Oak. This type of single malt is slowly gaining popularity. Distillers who traditionally reuse casks can experiment with this type of cask to see what it does to their spirit. Using a new cask results in more color and flavor being released rapidly, possibly changing the traditional flavor profile of an established whisky.

106. **What Is the Angels' Share?**

Oak casks and barrels breathe, which is why some of their content evaporates during maturation. The percentage of liquid that evaporates annually from a cask is called the angels' share. This number may vary depending on the location of the warehouse, so in Scotland, for example, one might see an evaporation percentage between 1.5 percent and 2.5 percent per year, while in hotter climates, like India, it may be as high as 12 percent.

During maturation in Scotland, the percentage of alcohol slowly decreases because more alcohol than water evaporates with the angels' share due to the relatively mild climate, the humidity level, and the relatively small changes in temperature between summer and winter.

107. What Is the Difference Between First Fill and Refill Casks?

First fill casks are those filled with spirit for the first time, after being used to store a different alcoholic liquid (like sherry or bourbon). When they've been used for spirit more than once, they become refill casks.

108. How Many Times Can a Barrel Be Used?

An oak needs to grow at least eighty years before it can efficiently be turned into planks of the desired thickness, porosity, and pliability for making a whisky barrel or cask.

Each cask will be used two or three times in its life, depending on how long each maturation cycle takes and where it's stored. A barrel for maturing straight bourbon can be used only one time for that purpose. Once in its lifetime, a cask can be rejuvenated by scraping the inside and recharring. The head and end are replaced as well. The Speyside Cooperage, one of Scotland's largest cooperages, uses this technique on many of their casks each year.

Reassembling a cask in the Speyside Cooperage, Scotland.

109. What Happens During Maturation?

During maturation, the liquid inside the cask expands when the temperature rises and contracts when it gets lower. This slow pulsating motion causes the liquid to take on the color, aroma, and flavor of the wood. A new cask will transfer more of its characteristics onto the whisky than a cask that has been used before. The wood, in turn, extracts aromas and flavors from the whisky, while the charred inside of the cask acts as a filter for impurities.

110. Does the Size of the Cask Influence the Maturation Process?

Yes—the smaller the cask, the greater the influence of the wood on the whisky. This has to do with the surface-to-volume ratio. Whisky matured in a quarter cask (125 liters) may develop as much flavor in six years as ten-year-old whisky maturing in a hogshead (250 liters).

111. Does Location Influence Maturation?

Both the microclimate affecting the geographical location of the warehouse as well as the location in the warehouse itself play a role during maturation. The higher in the warehouse the cask is stored, the higher the temperature and the more intense the interaction between wood and liquid. In Scotland the temperature in a warehouse remains relatively stable throughout the year, unlike in, for example, Kentucky or India, where temperatures can vary immensely between seasons. This is why a few distilleries use climate control units where temperatures are monitored and adjusted automatically. Humidity is another huge factor to take into account. Generally speaking, the drier the climate and the larger the temperature fluctuations, the more water evaporates from the whisky, producing a spirit with a higher alcohol content.

112. At What Alcohol Percentage Is Spirit Poured into the Cask?

Most whisky in Scotland is poured into the cask at 63.5 percent ABV, although higher percentages—up to 70 percent ABV—have been observed.

113. At What Alcohol Percentage Does Whisky Come Out of the Cask?

During maturation, the cask loses about 2 percent of its contents annually. This affects the ABV differently in different climates. In Scotland, where the humidity is relatively high and the temperature consistent, more alcohol than water evaporates by volume, so the longer the whisky matures, the lower the ABV gets. It's rare for Scotch whisky to leave the cask at the 63.5 percent ABV it entered at—58 percent ABV is more common. In Kentucky, the opposite is true: as a consequence of the

lower humidity and great fluctuations in temperature throughout the year, more water than alcohol evaporates. Whiskey might leave the barrel at 67 percent ABV or more. The master blender decides when it's time to bottle the whisky and at what strength, but in order to consider a spirit whisky, the minimum legal limit is 40 percent ABV. This regulation was introduced in Scotland and England at the turn of the nineteenth century in order to assure a standard of quality.

114. What Is Reracking?

The master blender monitors the spirit's quality throughout maturation by testing samples at regular intervals. If a whisky is not maturing as expected, the whisky will be reracked—transferred to another cask mid-cycle—in the hopes of achieving a better result. If a cask is showing signs of leakage that can't be repaired, the whisky will be reracked as well.

115. What Is Wood Finish or Extra Maturation?

When a whisky has been maturing in one type of cask for a long period of time and is then transferred into another type of cask for a short period before bottling, the procedure is called wood finish or extra maturation. This is done to add an extra layer of flavors to the whisky. Some whisky blenders use the term *marrying* to describe this process of adding additional flavors by way of extra maturation. Scottish Glenmorangie is a pioneer in this area (see images opposite).

Previous pages: Casks at Bunnahabhain Distillery, bordering the Sound of Islay.

116. Does the Wood Influence the Final Flavor of Whisky?

About 60 percent of whisky's taste is derived from the cask in which it matured, so, yes, the wood has a huge influence on taste. A poor-quality distillate cannot be improved in a fine cask, but a fine distillate can be ruined in a bad cask, the latter either being poorly manufactured or having off notes from previous contents that will negatively influence the taste and aroma of the eventual whisky.

From left: Matured in ex-bourbon casks; extra-matured in ex-sherry casks; extra-matured in ex-port casks; extra-matured in ex-sauternes casks.

117. How Many Single Malts Come from Scotland?

There are about 120 working distilleries in Scotland. However, every distillery makes various versions of their single malt and may give them different names. The Macallan, for example, produces a special series of single malts called Gold, Amber, Sienna, and Ruby. In chapter 9 you'll find a list of Scottish malt whisky distilleries with a map of their locations (see pages 278–85).

GRAIN WHISKY

118. How Is Grain Whisky Made?

Grain whisky is made of corn or wheat. The grain of choice is first cooked in an industrial pressure cooker, which softens the starch. A small amount of malted barley, rich in enzymes, is then added to convert the starch into fermentable sugars. The fermentation of this sugar-rich liquid is similar to pot still distillation. The wash enters a column still at a low ABV and leaves it as a fluid with a high alcohol content. This column distillation is usually done in two steps, using two connected columns.

119. What Is Column Distillation?

Contrary to pot still distillation, which is a batch-oriented process whereby the stills need to cool down and be cleaned after each round of distilling before being heated up again, column still distillation is a continuous process. One of the first column stills was designed by Aeneas Coffey, an Irish distiller, and patented in the first half of the nineteenth century. The structure usually consists of two interconnected columns, an analyzer and a rectifier. Both are divided into a series of compartments, separated by perforated plates.

120. How Does the Analyzer Work?

Wash, the low-alcohol fluid retained after fermentation, is fed into the column through a copper pipe attached to the top of the analyzer, where the wash is poured over the first perforated plate. The liquid starts to trickle through the compartments and makes its way to the bottom of the column while steam simultaneously rises from the bottom and ascends through the plates, making contact with the liquid and stripping it of alcohol.

121. How Does the Rectifier Work?

The alcoholic fumes travel from the analyzer through a pipe to the bottom of the rectifier and start ascending again. Since the various alcohols fractionate at different temperatures, the spirit divides into various parts. The heavier alcohols condense back into liquid form and lie on the plates. Only the lighter alcoholic vapors make it to the top of the column and are collected in a condenser. The eventual spirit contains approximately 90 to 94.8 percent ABV.

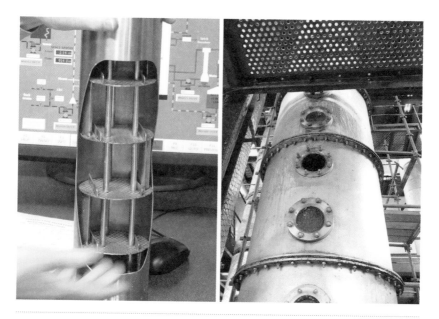

Opposite: The gigantic column stills at Girvan Distillery. *Above, left:* Scale model of the inside of a column still. *Above, right:* Column still at Cooley, Ireland.

---

122. How Does Grain Whisky Mature?

Most grain whisky matures in casks, previously used for bourbon, made of American white oak. As with malt whisky, the spirit has to mature at least three years before it can be considered whisky. The casks are stored in racked warehouses.

123. How Many Grain Distilleries Does Scotland Have?

Grain whisky in Scotland is made in huge quantities by seven large distilleries: Cameron Bridge, Girvan, Glen Turner/Starlaw, Invergordon, Loch Lomond, North British, and Strathclyde. The number of grain whisky distilleries used to be even greater and included some famous ones that have been closed or demolished, like Cambus, Dumbarton, Garnheath, and Port Dundas. Some of their whisky can still be found on the market today.

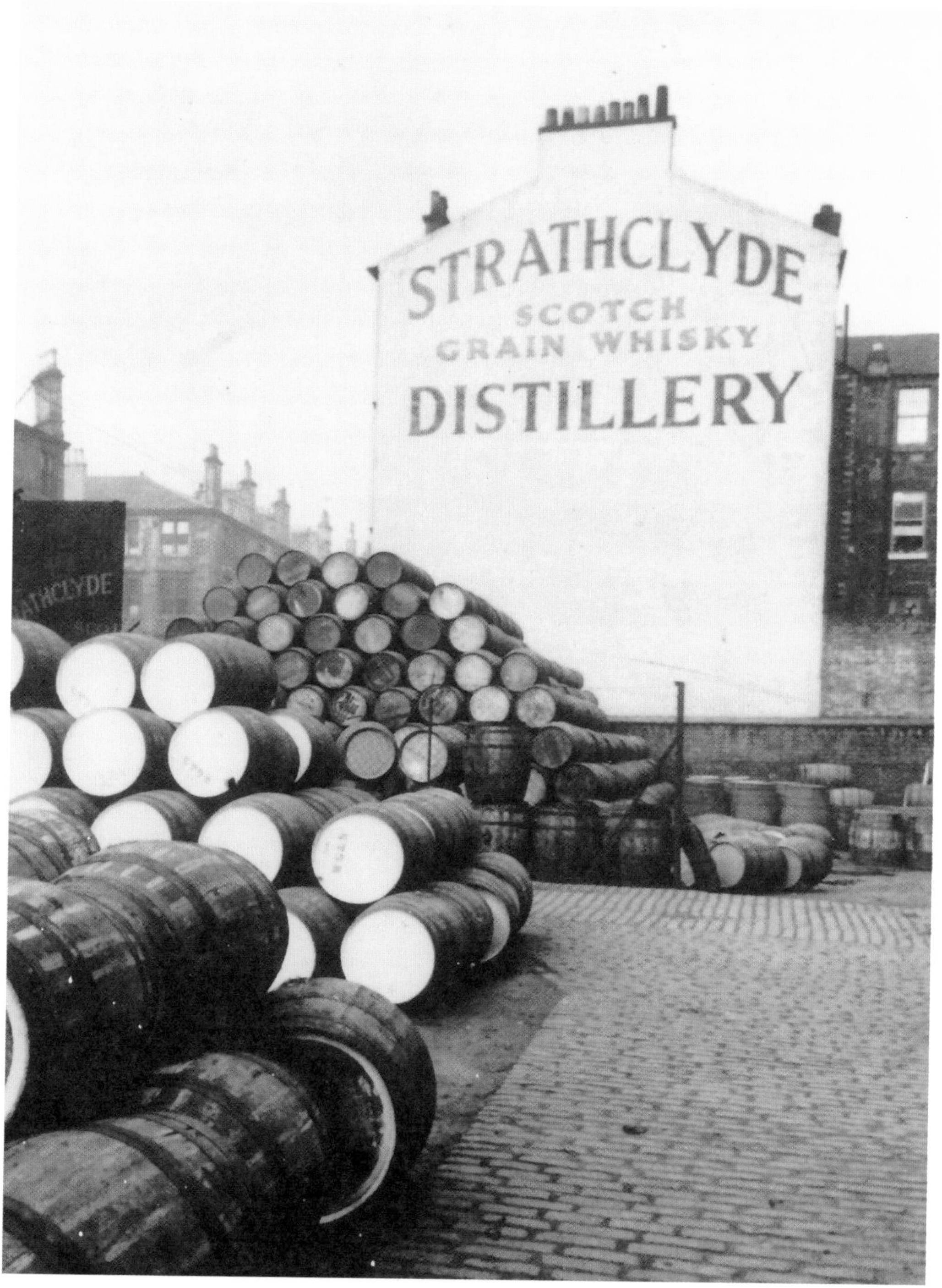
STRATHCLYDE
SCOTCH
GRAIN WHISKY
DISTILLERY
STRATHCLYDE

BLENDED WHISKY

124. How Is Blended Whisky Made?

Blended whisky is composed of various mature whiskies. The backbone of a blended Scotch whisky is always a grain whisky, made from either corn or wheat, in a column still. After maturation, a percentage of mature single malts is added to create a particular flavor profile. The flavor and composition are unique to each blend, and the recipe is a secret of the master blender. Blending is sometimes compared to composing a symphony—each whisky plays its part and contributes its own note to the end product, making the whole greater than the sum of its parts.

125. How Do You Make a Good Blend?

To create a good blend, the master blender regularly tests samples from various casks of single malt whiskies to analyze how they develop over time. For this, he predominantly uses his sense of smell. A liquid library of samples is created to ensure that different components of the flavor remain easily identifiable.

The blender is extremely knowledgeable about the difference in taste of each malt whisky and can effortlessly find an adequate replacement should a certain brand temporarily run out of stock. A handy tool of the trade is a malt classification system widely embraced by the industry. It can be found in Richard Paterson's excellent book *Goodness Nose*. Finally, choosing the right casks is key to a successful blend. Distilling whisky is a craft; blending whisky is an art.

Rachel Barrie in her blending lab.

126. How Many Blends Are There?

Some of the well-known brands of blended whisky are Johnnie Walker, Ballantine's, The Famous Grouse, Chivas, Dewar's, White Horse, Black & White, and Cutty Sark, but countless others have been developed over the past 150 years. Most of the blends got their names from small family enterprises founded in the second part of the nineteenth century, when blending became legal. Apart from these household names, many cleverly named blends appear on store shelves. They are made to order, tailored to the customer's specifications, all following a different recipe. In countries that allow liquor to be sold in supermarkets, it is not unusual to see a house blend specially developed for certain chains of stores.

127. Who Was Andrew Usher?

This Scottish wine and liquor merchant is considered the father of blended whisky. He was one of the first whisky producers who took advantage of a change in British law around 1860 that allowed blending distillates made from different grains. According to legend, Usher's mother taught him how to create whisky blends at her kitchen table.

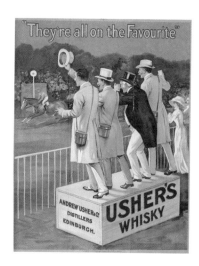

128. Who Was Johnnie Walker?

John Walker owned a grocery shop in Kilmarnock, Scotland, in the 1820s. When the shop was severely damaged by a flood, John's son Alexander turned a disaster into a fortune by turning the company into a whisky wholesale business. To create a name for the brand in other parts of the world, Alexander Walker made deals with ship captains in Glasgow Harbour. They would transport his whisky to the far corners of the world and receive part of the profit in

exchange. One century later, Johnnie Walker Red Label had become one of the best-known blended whiskies in the world. Peter Brown designed the famous logo of the striding man in 1908. Sometimes he marches from left to right, other times from right to left.

129. Who Was George Ballantine?

Archibald Ballantine was a farmer from Peebles in the Scottish Borders region. When his son George turned thirteen, he brought him to Edinburgh, where the boy was to apprentice with grocery and wine merchant Andrew Hunter. Six years later, in 1887, George opened his own grocery store in Cowgate, near Edinburgh Castle. From there he built an empire that was eventually acquired by Pernod Ricard, a French beverage company.

George was good friends with whisky distiller Andrew Usher and learned a lot about blending whisky from him. George put Ballantine's on the Scottish market, while his sons Archibald and George Junior developed the brand further in Edinburgh and Glasgow, respectively. When Queen Victoria honored the company with a Royal Warrant at the turn of the nineteenth century, the brand was propelled to international fame.

130. Where Does the Name *Famous Grouse* Originate?

In 1869, Matthew Gloag & Son, founded in 1800, launched a blended Scotch named The Grouse. Soon it was so successful that people started referring to it as the *famous* Grouse. Gloag appropriately registered this trade name on August 12, 1905, or "the Glorious Twelfth," which refers to the start of grouse season in Great Britain. The brand is steeped in tradition, and the descendants of the founding family are still involved with the business. The logo is derived from an original drawing, supposedly done by the founder's aunt. The bird was stylized regularly over time.

131. **Who Were the Chivas Brothers?**

Brothers John and James Chivas left their parents' farm in 1836 to try their luck near Aberdeen, Scotland. It took two years before James was hired as an assistant in Edward's Grocery Store on King Street. The shop was popular among the town's elite because of its wide range of products. After James became a partner in the company, he hired his brother and they became passionate about providing the highest-quality products. The brothers expanded the business with catering facilities, and soon they were purchasing whisky by the cask. Both brothers had excellent noses, and their premium blend Chivas Regal took off worldwide. They were bought out by Canadian company Seagram around 1950, which brought Chivas Regal to an even larger stage. The shop in Aberdeen doesn't exist anymore, but the name lives on, as a whisky and as a company, since current owner Pernod Ricard consolidated all its whisky distilleries, including the beautiful old Strathisla in Keith, under the name Chivas Brothers Ltd.

CHIVAS BROTHERS LTD.
DISTILLERS
ABERDEEN SCOTLAND

The oldest malt whisky distillery in the Highlands of Scotland, Strathisla Glenlivet Distillery, established in 1786, is owned and operated by Chivas Brothers Ltd. The finest and most treasured product of this old house is "CHIVAS REGAL WHISKY," matured in oak casks for fully 12 years and representing a century and a half of experience in producing fine Scotch Whisky.

132. **Who Was Tommy Dewar?**

The Dewar's brand was built by John Alexander and Tommy, sons of founder John Dewar. While John held down the fort in Scotland, younger brother Tommy embarked on a world tour. With his flamboyant appearance, Tommy managed to make Dewar's known worldwide within twenty years. During his travels, he wrote a book called *A Ramble Round the Globe*. He also dabbled in politics and was appointed sheriff of London more than once. The term *Dewarism* was coined in honor of his witty one-liners.

133. What Do the Initials in *J&B* Represent?

The story of this brand hides a great romance at its origins. Giacomo Justerini, son of an Italian distiller, was absolutely mesmerized by Italian soprano Margherita Bellino's performance and fell in love with her. In 1749 he followed her to England, and although their love didn't last, his knack for business did. He became a successful wine and spirit merchant in London, selling the business to his partner after eleven years and returning to Italy. In 1831 the well-established company was sold to Alfred Brooks, who renamed it Justerini & Brooks. Around 1884 the company started to lay down stocks of whisky and had a blend created: J&B Club, the forerunner of J&B Rare blended Scotch whisky. This light and smooth blend is excellent in a cocktail.

134. Where Does the Name *Black & White* Originate?

James Buchanan was Tommy Dewar's biggest rival—not only as a whisky maker but also as a fan of horse racing. Both men owned a considerable stable of thoroughbreds. When Buchanan introduced a new blend featuring a white label with his name printed in black letters, it did not take long for customers to ask for the "Black and White." A Scottie and a Westie, the canine mascots of the brand, were added to the label many years later. Buchanan was one of the first whisky barons to deliver whisky exclusively to the House of Lords, the upper house of British Parliament.

James Buchanan

135. Who Is Behind the White Horse Label?

White Horse is a legendary Scottish blend named after a famous pub in Edinburgh, the White Horse Cellar Inn. There is more than a drop of Lagavulin single malt in the White Horse. Not surprisingly so, since both brands and distilleries were once owned by the same man, Peter Mackie. Restless Peter, as he was nicknamed, was energetic and highly competitive and came with a short fuse. For a long time, he quarreled with his neighbor Laphroaig, whose single malt had been represented by the Mackie family for many years. When Laphroaig one-sidedly ended

the agreement, Mackie went through the roof and tried to make life as difficult as possible for the man he used to do business with. He even tried to copy Laphroaig's whisky by building a second, smaller distillery called Malt Mill within his main distillery, Lagavulin. He did not succeed, but his blend White Horse is still in existence and is currently owned by Diageo.

136. What Is the Story Behind Cutty Sark?

"Tam o' Shanter" is one of Robert Burns's most famous poems. It served as the inspiration for a whisky brand created and launched in 1923. The poem, written in 1790, includes a paragraph describing poor Tam being pursued by a fast-running wild witch wearing a short nightgown known as a cutty sark. Almost eighty years later, in 1870, Captain Jock Willis used the name for his new tea clipper, designed to sail unusually fast for its time. Its maiden trip brought the *Cutty Sark* from London to Shanghai, and the ship would complete eight such expeditions, becoming famous in its own right.

In 1923, London-based wine and whisky merchant Berry Brothers & Rudd wanted to launch a new blended, easy-drinking whisky in the United States (mind you, this was during Prohibition!) and hired a Scottish artist, James McBey, to come up with a catchy name. Since the ship had been in the news constantly, Cutty Sark was an obvious choice. From then on it was smooth sailing for the blend.

137. What Other Scottish Blends Are Available?

There are countless Scottish blends, but the following is a non-exhaustive list—in alphabetical order—of blends that are available worldwide: the Antiquary, Bell's, Ben Alder, Black Bottle, Black Cock, Black Prince, Black Watch, Blue Hanger, BNJ, Buchanan's, Campbeltown Loch, Catto's, Clan Campbell, Clan MacGregor, Claymore, Crawford's, Dimple, Grant's Family Reserve, Haig, Hanky Bannister, High Commissioner, Highland Queen, Islay Mist, Lang's, Long John, Mackinlay, Old Parr, 100 Pipers, Passport, Pig's Nose, Sheep Dip, Six Isles, Stewart's Cream of the Barley, Teacher's, Té Bheag, the Talisman, Vat 69, Whyte and Mackay, William Lawson's, and Ye Monks.

PRODUCT OF SCOTLAND
Finest
PIG'S NOSE
Scotch Whisky
In Gloucestershire 'tis said that
our Scotch is as soft and as smooth as a pig's nose.
100% Scotch Whiskies Blended and bottled in Scotland
75 cl   40% vol
M.J.Dowdeswell & Co Ltd Oldbury-on-Severn Gloucestershire

Teacher's
EXTRA SPECIAL
OLD SCOTCH
Whisky
W^M TEACHER & SONS. L^TD
·GLASGOW·

THE
CLAYMORE
SCOTCH
WHISKY
DISTILLED, BLENDED AND BOTTLED IN SCOTLAND
A. FERGUSON & COMPANY, GLASGOW G2 5RG
70cl ℮   40%Vol

ESTD   1893
HIGHLAND QUEEN
FINE OLD SCOTCH WHISKY
PRODUCE OF SCOTLAND
Macdonald & Muir Ltd
DISTILLERS   LEITH   SCOTLAND
BOTTLED IN SCOTLAND

"THE BAILIE"
THE BAILIE NICOL JARVIE BLEND
→ OF ←
Old Scotch Whisky
PRODUCE OF
SCOTLAND
Sole Proprietors.
NICOL ANDERSON & CO., L^TD
43 OXFORD STREET.
GLASGOW.
PRE-WAR STRENGTH 25% U.P.
SPECIAL.   REG. NO. 35665.

ESTABLISHED
GLASGOW 1844 SCOTLAND
WHYTE AND MACKAY
SCOTCH WHISKY
JAMES
WHYTE   CHARLES
MACKAY
MATURED TWICE
Whyte & Mackay
DISTILLED, BLENDED
& BOTTLED IN SCOTLAND
70 cl ℮   40% vol
PRODUCT OF
SCOTLAND

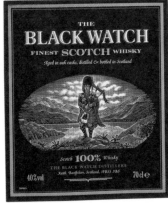

THE
BLACK WATCH
FINEST SCOTCH WHISKY
Aged in oak casks, distilled & bottled in Scotland
Scotch 100% Whisky
THE BLACK WATCH DISTILLERS
Keith, Banffshire, Scotland, AB55 5BS
40% vol   70 cl ℮

TRADE MARK
ESTD. 1860
CRAWFORD'S
★ ★ ★
SPECIAL RESERVE
OLD SCOTCH WHISKY
DISTILLED, BLENDED AND BOTTLED IN SCOTLAND.
A.A.Crawford & Co
A.A. CRAWFORD & CO. GLASGOW G2 5RG, SCOTLAND.
75 cl   40%Vol.

ONE QUART 86 PROOF

100% SCOTCH WHISKIES 100% SCOTCH WHISKIES

100 PIPERS
BLENDED SCOTCH WHISKY

DISTILLED, BLENDED AND BOTTLED IN SCOTLAND
GLEN KEITH-GLENLIVET DISTILLERY CO. LTD.
DISTILLERS KEITH, SCOTLAND

CATTO'S
RARE OLD SCOTTISH
Highland Whisky

JAMES CATTO & Co LTD, AIRDRIE, SCOTLAND
Distilled, Blended and Bottled in Scotland
Produit et embouteillé en Écosse.

750ml 40% alc/vol

100% SCOTCH WHISKIES

CAMPBELTOWN LOCH

BLENDED
SCOTCH WHISKY

DISTILLED, BLENDED & BOTTLED BY
SPRINGBANK DISTILLERS LTD. CAMPBELTOWN · SCOTLAND

70cl PRODUCT OF SCOTLAND 40% vol

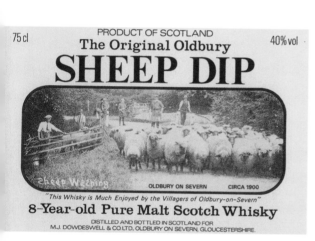

75 cl PRODUCT OF SCOTLAND 40% vol

The Original Oldbury
SHEEP DIP

Sheep Washing OLDBURY ON SEVERN CIRCA 1900

"This Whisky is Much Enjoyed by the Villagers of Oldbury-on-Severn"

8-Year-old Pure Malt Scotch Whisky

DISTILLED AND BOTTLED IN SCOTLAND FOR
M.J. DOWDESWELL & CO.LTD, OLDBURY ON SEVERN, GLOUCESTERSHIRE.

40% vol PRODUCT OF SCOTLAND 75 cl

BEN ALDER

FINEST
SCOTCH WHISKY

BLENDED & BOTTLED BY
GORDON & MACPHAIL
ELGIN · SCOTLAND

Clan MacGregor
Fine Scotch Whisky

ESTᴰ 1709

THIS SIGNATURE IS OUR GUARANTEE OF AUTHENTICITY

J·G·THOMSON & Cᴼ LTᴰ
GLASGOW
PRODUCT OF SCOTLAND

0%Vol 70cl e

PRODUCT OF SCOTLAND

GLEN TALLOCH
- CHOICE -

BLENDED
SCOTCH WHISKY

ALC 40%VOL. 1.0Lℓ

Distilled and shipped by
Crammond & Sons

ISLAY MIST

THE GREAT SEAL OF ISLAY

750ml 40% alc/vol

Deluxe

BLENDED SCOTCH WHISKY

DISTILLED, BLENDED AND BOTTLED IN SCOTLAND
MACDUFF INTERNATIONAL LIMITED

138. Why Are There So Many Blended Whiskies?

Between the seventeenth and nineteenth centuries, a true cottage industry developed in the Scottish Highlands. Hundreds of farmers-turned-distillers made their own expressions of single malt whisky. Export to the Lowlands or England was virtually nonexistent, since the population of the southern part of Great Britain preferred brandy (cognac) or gin. During the nineteenth century, five important events reshaped the Scottish whisky landscape and in its wake the consumption pattern among the English.

1. The Invention of the Column Still

In 1827, Irish distiller Robert Stein patented a still that made continuous distillation possible. It wasn't a pot still such as the Highlanders in Scotland used, but a several-foot-high column. Another Irishman, named Aeneas Coffey, improved the column and registered a patent for his idea in 1830. The column still, sometimes referred to as a Coffey still, was born. From that moment on, it was possible to distill alcohol from various types of grains on a large industrial scale. The Irish distillers didn't like the invention and ignored it, whereas the Scottish Lowlanders embraced the new distilling device. They used it to make huge amounts of cheap grain whisky, less outspoken in flavor than the distinctive and more expensive malt whiskies from the Highlands, which at the time often had smoky or medicinal notes.

2. Law Changes

The second event was the 1846 repeal of the Corn Laws. Up to that point, distillers were allowed to use only barley for making whisky, but the new law allowed for cheaper grains, like corn and wheat, to be used for distilling alcohol. In 1860, another breakthrough came in the form of a law change in Scotland that allowed the blending of different distillates made from different base materials. Andrew Usher was among the first to see an excellent opportunity for increasing his market share and became the de facto "father of blending." Usher purchased casks of single malts from individual Highlands distillers and blended their product with cheap grain alcohol. He also blended malt whiskies with one another, calling the end product Usher's Old Vatted Glenlivet (sometimes spelled Glenlivat). It did not take long before other wine and liquor merchants followed his example. The Chivas Brothers started their blending business in Aberdeen, and John Dewar and Alexander Bell followed suit in Perth. William Teacher was running his blending business in Glasgow, and elsewhere John Walker, George Ballantine, Robert Haig, Matthew Gloag, and James Buchanan practiced the art of blending whisky. Most of these family names live on as famous whisky brands today.

"WHISKY IS LIQUID SUNSHINE."

George Bernard Shaw

3. A Disaster in France

The third event took place in France. In 1863 a blight plagued the French vineyards and decimated nearly half of them within two decades. The disease was caused by a nasty bug accidentally imported from America, the *Phylloxera vastratix*. Cognac became scarce and expensive, and the English had to look elsewhere for their tipple of choice. They found an alternative in the new drink being produced at home—blended whisky. The drink became an instant success, envied by the Highlanders, with their distinctive single malts.

PHYLLOXERA

4. Compromised Quality

The fourth event was a crime. At the turn of the nineteenth century, whisky consumption was booming and some blenders cut corners in an attempt to optimize their profits, which inevitably compromised the quality of the product. The Pattison brothers caused a huge stir in the Scottish whisky industry when it was discovered that they had doctored their drink by mixing immature grain whisky with fine single malts and promoted it as a premium whisky and largely inflated their profits. The Pattisons were found guilty of fraud and sent to prison. Around 1917, their wrongdoings led to a law in which Scotch whisky was defined in new, stricter terms—it had to mature for at least three years in oak casks and had to be bottled at a minimum of 40 percent ABV. This quality control facilitated acceptance and appreciation of blended Scotch whisky among consumers.

Opposite: Pattisons' ad.

5. International Conquest

Blended whisky performed well outside of Scotland and England as a replacement for cognac. When famous jazz musicians and Hollywood movie stars openly pledged their allegiance to Scotch, its export grew in an unprecedented way. Various blends became "rock stars" in their own right. Dewar's still is one of the bestselling blends in the United States, and Johnnie Walker is the number one bestseller worldwide in the blended whisky category. Sometimes it seems that single malt whisky plays the main role in the whisky world, but numbers and figures show a different story. More than 85 percent of all Scotch whisky sold around the planet is of the blended variety. Today the famous brands are no longer owned by the founding families. Save one or two, they have all been bought by the larger companies like Bacardi (Dewar's), Diageo (Bell's and Johnnie Walker), Beam Suntory (Teacher's), and Pernod Ricard (Chivas and Ballantine's). Many of these big conglomerates own grain distilleries as well as great numbers of single malt distilleries. That is a strategic choice, because those who want to create a beautiful blended whisky need access to a regular, reliable supply of single malts. Therefore, these multinational companies regularly swap casks with one another without compensation, to offer their own master blenders a greater palate of choices. This is where single malt and grain whisky meet.

Opposite: A bottle of Haig blended scotch in the dressing room of jazz pianist Fats Waller (1904–43).

IRISH WHISKEY

139. How Is Irish Whiskey Made?

The Irish, credited by many as the inventors of whiskey, produce single malts as well as single grains and blends. Their *mode d'emploi* is similar to that of their Scottish neighbors, although they rarely use peat smoke for drying the malt. An exception to that rule is the smoky Connemara, produced at Cooley Distillery. But there is one specific category exclusively made in Ireland—single pot still whiskey.

140. What Is Single Pot Still Whiskey?

The Irish saw an increase in taxes on malted barley in the nineteenth century. To cut costs, the large Irish distillers decided to use a greater percentage of unmalted barley, mixing it with the malted variety. Currently, the usual ratio is 60:40 in favor of unmalted barley, but the percentages can vary per brand. This particular balance gives traditional Irish single pot still whiskey its distinctive spicy-apple-linseed character and its smooth, oily body.

Opposite, above: The former Jameson Distillery in Dublin now houses a beautiful whiskey museum. *Opposite, below:* Cooley's pot stills.

141. How Is Single Pot Still Whiskey Made?

Traditional Irish single pot still whiskey is triple distilled in pot stills. The first round takes place in the wash still, usually aided by a column to promote reflux. The spirit is rid of its heavier elements and collected at 25 percent ABV for the heavier expressions, and at 38 percent ABV for the lighter ones, depending on what style of whiskey the distiller is going for. In the second, intermediate (or feints) still, the stream of alcohol is separated. The weaker feints (between 45 and 47 percent ABV) are caught and redistilled into heavy spirit. The stronger feints (between 75 and 85 percent) produce a lighter spirit. The spirit still works as a regular still in which only the heart of the run is used for making the eventual whiskey. Since Irish distillers produce a large variety of spirits, the distilling regimen varies accordingly—with different filling levels and cut points in the intermediate and spirit stills.

142. What Is Potcheen?

"Illegally" produced whiskey—without a legally acquired license and its associated regulations—is called "potcheen," whereas the legal product is sometimes referred to by the tongue-in-cheek term *parliament whiskey*. Potcheen (also spelled as "poitín") is colorless and not matured. It is often consumed in secret, but you can also find it bottled on the shelf in a liquor store. This is, in fact, the legally produced spirit from a legal distillery, but it cannot be called whiskey due to its lack of cask maturation.

143. How Does Irish Whiskey Mature?

The Irish distillers rarely use dunnage warehouses. Most Irish whiskey matures in racked warehouses where the casks are palletized in an upright position. A variety of casks are used, some of which may have previously held other liquids, such as sherry, port, bourbon, and Madeira, but the majority of the spirit is poured into first fill casks.

144. How Many Irish Distilleries Are There?

The Irish economy had to overcome many adversities in the second half of the nineteenth century and the beginning of the twentieth: the Great Potato Famine, Prohibition in the United States, the 1929 Wall Street Crash and its worldwide rippling effects, and economic wars with England. As a result, the Irish whiskey industry was reduced from a major force into a marginal player on the world market. Closures and mergers ensued, resulting in only two companies left standing: Irish Distillers in the Irish Republic and Bushmills in Northern Ireland.

Cooley joined the ranks in 1989, becoming a forerunner of the industry upsurge in the decades that followed. As of today, more than twelve distilleries throughout both countries have caused the phoenix that is Irish whiskey to rise from the ashes with a new lease on life (a map of all their locations can be found on page 287). Irish Distillers (owned by Pernod Ricard) and Cooley/Kilbeggan (owned by Beam Suntory) are still the major players in the Republic, as is Bushmills (owned by Jose Cuervo) in Northern Ireland.

Opposite: The decommissioned pot stills of Powers: an industrial monument gracing the courtyard of this former distillery in Dublin. The buildings now house the National College of Art and Design.

145. What Are the Well-Known Irish Whiskey Brands?

Jameson has been the market leader among Irish blended whiskey for a long time. Tullamore Dew, the original ingredient in Irish coffee, takes second place. Other far-reaching brands are Bushmills/Black Bush (malt whiskey and blended whiskey), Powers (blend and single pot still), Paddy (blend), Redbreast and Green Spot (single pot still), Kilbeggan (blended and grain), and Connemara and Tyrconnell (single malts). One of my personal favorites is Writers Tears, a pot still blend.

Opposite: In the village of Kilbeggan stands the oldest working distillery in Ireland. Founded as Brusna and later known as Locke's, currently the distillery carries the same name as the village.

BOURBON

146. How Is Bourbon Made?

Bourbon is made from a mixture of grains consisting of at least 51 percent corn, with the addition of rye and/or wheat and malted barley. The corn adds a fatty sweetness to the distillate and provides the "backbone" of the drink. A small portion of malted barley promotes the formation of enzymes needed to convert the starch into sugars: the wheat will make the bourbon softer and smoother, whereas rye will give the drink a spicier character. Wheat and rye are called "flavor grains," and the corn-to-flavor-grains ratio has a huge impact on the aroma and taste of the end product.

Clockwise from top left: corn; rye; barley; wheat.

147. **What Is a Mash Bill?**

The mash bill is a recipe showing the percentage of grains used for a specific bourbon. Distilleries often use more than one mash bill and in doing so can create a huge variety of bourbons. Most distillers carefully keep their mash bills a secret. Not the case with Four Roses, a company that uses two different recipes: "OB," containing 60 percent corn, 35 percent rye, and 5 percent malted barley; and "OE," with the ratio of the same ingredients at 75 percent, 20 percent, and 5 percent. Maker's Mark is known for using wheat instead of rye as its flavor grain. Its mash bill is 70 percent corn, 16 percent red winter wheat, and 14 percent malted barley.

148. **What Is a Mash Cooker?**

A mash cooker is a kind of a pressure cooker. After the corn has been milled and mixed with water, it goes into the mash cooker. When it's done cooking, it's cooled and rye and/or wheat are added to it. This mixture is cooked at a lower temperature and cooled down a second time. Only then is the small percentage of malted barley added.

Opposite: The mash cooker at Buffalo Trace in Frankfort, Kentucky.

"TELL ME WHAT BRAND OF WHISKEY
GENERAL GRANT DRINKS. I WOULD
LIKE TO SEND A BARREL OF IT TO
MY OTHER GENERALS."

Abraham Lincoln

149. **What Is Sour Mash?**

Most bourbons are made with sour mash. This is the by-product of a distillation round in the form of an acidic liquid that is added to the next batch during fermentation. Sour mash keeps the pH value at the desired level and keeps bacteria at bay. The amount of added sour mash influences the percentage of sugars in the mash—when trying to achieve a fresh and light bourbon, less sour mash is added.

At Woodford Reserve in Versailles, Kentucky, the mash cooker and the fermentation vessels are in the same room.

150. What Are Fermenters?

Fermenters are yeast vessels (they're called washbacks in Scotland). They are made from wood, as well as stainless steel. Most distillers in the United States use a proprietary yeast strain that is kept alive at the distillery. One strain is common, but some distillers use two, three, or more. For example, Four Roses is famous for using five different yeast strains. Fermentation takes up to three days, resulting in a "beer" containing 5 to 6 percent ABV.

The fermenters in the large bourbon distilleries are gigantic vessels, like this one at Buffalo Trace in Frankfort, Kentucky.

151. **What Happens in the Beer Still?**

The "beer" from the fermenter is distilled in a single column still. It is poured in from the top; steam enters the column at the bottom. The beer trickles through perforated plates on its way down and meets the ascending steam that strips it of alcohol. These alcoholic fumes then condense into a liquid containing 55 to 60 percent alcohol. A second distilling round may take place in a piece of equipment called a thumper or a doubler, depending on the type.

152. **What Is a Thumper?**

A thumper is a huge copper kettle containing water. The alcohol fumes pass through it. Heavier elements are withdrawn and the liquid is purified, while concentrating the alcohol even further. The equipment takes its name from the thumping sound the kettle makes when it's working.

153. **What Is a Doubler?**

Instead of a thumper, a doubler might be used for the second round of distillation. It somewhat resembles a pot still and works similarly (see entry 64).

154. **What Are Heads and Tails?**

Heads and tails are the equivalents of foreshots and feints in single malt whisky production (see entries 78 and 80).

Opposite: The beer still at Four Roses, Lawrenceburg, Kentucky.

155. What Is the Tail Box?

The tail box is the equivalent of the spirit safe in a single malt whisky distillery (see entry 77).

156. What Is White Dog?

White dog is the colorless liquid that comes from the still before it is poured into a barrel. By law, white dog cannot be more than 80 percent ABV, and most distillers stay far under that percentage. The less alcohol, the oilier the white dog.

157. How Long Does Bourbon Mature?

There is no legal minimum number of years for bourbon to mature. The distillate may be called bourbon one day after it has left the still. Straight bourbon, which is more regulated, needs to mature at least two years (see entry 166).

158. What Kind of Barrel Is Used for Bourbon Maturation?

In the United States, a distillate can be called bourbon only when it has matured in brand-new charred barrels made of American white oak.

Clockwise from top left: This thumper belongs to Wild Turkey Distillery in Lawrenceburg, Kentucky; the doubler at Four Roses used for the second distillation; in front of Four Roses' tail box stands a glass of white dog.

159. What Types of Warehouses Are Used for Maturing Bourbon?

Most warehouses in the United States are many stories high and equipped with wooden or steel racks. The exterior is often clad in corrugated iron, but some are brick buildings, such as the warehouse at Buffalo Trace, in Frankfort, Kentucky, where the famous single barrel bourbon Blanton's matures. Four Roses uses very low-rise buildings—barrels can be stacked only six high.

The characteristic red shutters on the black warehouses at Maker's Mark, Loretto, Kentucky.

160. Does Bourbon Have an Angels' Share?

In the warehouses, especially in Kentucky, temperatures are very high in the summer and low in the winter, whereas the humidity is relatively low. Because of these climate conditions, more water evaporates than alcohol. It is remarkable, but after maturation, the ABV of the bourbon that comes out of the barrel may be higher than that of the white dog that entered it years earlier. So bourbon does have its angels' share (see entry 106), but it contains less alcohol than it would in Scotland. Guess which country the angels favor!

A warehouse owned by Heaven Hill faces the entrance of the Bourbon Heritage Center in Bardstown, Kentucky.

161. **What Is Barrel Dumping?**

As soon as the master distiller has decided which barrels are ready for bottling, they are emptied into a large stainless steel gutter. This is called barrel dumping. The contents are filtered and diluted until the desired ABV percentage is reached. The contents need to be filtered because each barrel releases a small amount of charcoal along with the mature bourbon (a result of the barrel charring that was done before it was used).

While dumping a barrel of Woodford Reserve, the distillery manager takes a sample to check the quality of the bourbon.

162. **What Is the Devil's Cut?**

When the barrel is dumped, a small amount of whiskey will stay behind in the wood. This is called the devil's cut (the antithesis to the angels' share—see entry 106). Jim Beam has developed a method by which the residue can be rinsed out of the barrel. They use the rinsing water to dilute one of its bourbons, called Devil's Cut.

163. Who Was the First Whiskey Distiller in the United States?

The answer to who really was the first distiller remains a matter of debate to this day. George Thorpe is believed to have made a distillate from corn near Jamestown in 1619. Evan Williams in 1783 is a possible candidate too. Elijah Craig (who supposedly started to distill whiskey in 1789) is often dubbed the father of bourbon, but without a shred of evidence. Both Williams and Craig have a bourbon named after them.

164. Is All American Whiskey Bourbon?

Not all American whiskey is bourbon, but all bourbon is American. Originally, American whiskey was made mainly of rye. It wasn't until later that the colonists began to distill domestic corn. American settlers claimed that the corn was given to them by Native Americans. Native Americans tell a different story: that the Pilgrim Fathers stole their hidden stock.

165. Does Bourbon Always Have to Come from Kentucky?

Bourbon can be made anywhere in the United States. The state of Kentucky has been the hub of bourbon production for decades.

166. What Is Straight Bourbon?

Production of straight bourbon has a far stricter rulebook than regular bourbon. These rules are described in the Federal Standards of Identity for Distilled Spirits (27.C.F.R.5). In short:

* The product has to be manufactured in the United States of America.

* The product has to be made of a mixture of grains, containing at least 51 percent corn.

* The product has to be matured in new oak barrels, charred from the inside.

* The distillate running from the still can be no more than 160 proof (80 percent ABV).

* When pumped into a barrel, the distillate can be no more than 125 proof (62.5 percent ABV).

* The bottled product should be at least 80 proof (40 percent ABV).

* Maturation time has to be at least two years.

* Adding of coloring agents, artificial flavor compounds, or other distillates is not allowed.

♦ When maturation has taken less than four years, the age has to be mentioned on the label.

♦ When an age is mentioned on the label, it should always be the youngest whiskey in the bottle.

167. What Is Kentucky Straight Bourbon?

When "Kentucky Straight Bourbon" is on the label, the whiskey in the bottle has to be made and matured in the Commonwealth of Kentucky. Maturation cannot be less than two years and one day.

168. Where Does the Name *Bourbon* Originate?

After the Revolutionary War, America baptized many counties and cities with French names, as a token of gratitude for the help received from France against the English. Kentucky's Bourbon County was named after the French royal family at the time. The whiskey distilled in that county was transported to Louisiana by boat. The product was very much welcomed down South, and customers started asking for "that whiskey from Bourbon County," which was eventually abbreviated to Bourbon.

On May 4, 1964, the U.S. Congress recognized bourbon as "a distinctive product of the United States." Since that date, bourbon could be made anywhere in the United States.

169. Does Bourbon Always Come from the United States?

Bourbon is officially an American product. However, this does not mean that bourbon cannot be made outside the United States. It just can't legally be called bourbon; "bourbon-style whisk(e)y" is used instead.

Jim Beam's small batch bourbon series (also see entry 213).

170. Why Is Jack Daniel's Tennessee Whiskey Not Called Bourbon?

Although the method of production is very similar to that of bourbon, Jack Daniel's styles itself as "Tennessee Whiskey." Unlike with bourbon, Jack Daniel's white dog is filtered through a thick layer of sugar maple charcoal before it is poured into a barrel.

Left: This wooden vessel is filled to the brim with charcoal. Jack's white dog trickles through this layer for days before maturing in oak barrels.
Right: A display dedicated to Jack Daniel, founder and namesake to one of the world's most famous distilleries and brands, located at the visitor center in Lynchburg, Tennessee.

171. What Is the Lincoln County Process?

This is a technique used in the production of Tennessee whiskey—the white dog is filtered through ten feet of sugar maple charcoal right before the liquid goes into the barrel for maturation. Charcoal filtering is an old technique used in ancient Russia for making vodka. The process in the United States gets its name from Lincoln County, which is where the Jack Daniel's Distillery was located when it was built. The county borders were later changed, and the distillery now resides in Moore County. Remarkably, the Alcohol and Tobacco Tax and Trade Bureau (TTB) has not yet made a rule that whiskey made in this fashion cannot be called bourbon. George Dickel makes Tennessee whiskey too.

The distillery of George Dickel is located in Tullahoma, Tennessee, a half-hour drive from the Jack Daniel's Distillery.

172. How Is Rye Whiskey Made?

Rye whiskey is made the same way as bourbon, except that the mash bill has at least 51 percent rye in the recipe.

173. How Long Does Rye Whiskey Mature?

There are no legal requirements regarding maturation time for rye whiskey.

174. How Is Wheat Whiskey Made?

Wheat whiskey is made the same way as bourbon, except that the mash bill has at least 51 percent wheat in the recipe.

175. How Long Must Wheat Whiskey Mature?

There are no legal requirements regarding maturation time for wheat whiskey.

176. Can Single Malt Whisk(e)y Be Made in the United States?

Single malt whisk(e)y can be made anywhere in the world. Various brands are produced in the United States, including McCarthy's Single Malt Whiskey. It is manufactured at Clear Creek Distillery in Portland, Oregon, and spelled with an "e."

177. What Are the Famous Bourbon Brands?

Prohibition in the United States, from 1920 to 1933, nearly killed the entire American whiskey industry. After its repeal, a small group, located mainly in Kentucky, started to rebuild the industry. Five among them currently produce the lion's share of Kentucky bourbon. Some famous brands are Blanton's, Buffalo Trace, Elijah Craig, Four Roses, Heaven Hill, Jim Beam, Maker's Mark, Old Forester, Wild Turkey, and Woodford Reserve, which is triple distilled in pot stills that were built in Scotland—a unique feature in the bourbon industry.

The stopper of Blanton's Single Barrel is a racehorse figurine—a symbol of the Kentucky Derby, a race held annually in Louisville, Kentucky, on the first Saturday in May. The horse figurine comes in eight different poses. When combined, they show a racehorse in full stride. The hind leg of the horse is always engraved with one of the letters spelling "Blanton's": it's a real collectors' item.

178. **Prohibition in the United States**

In June 1919, Andrew J. Volstead proposed a radical law that would shake up the American economy. Later that year, it passed in both the House and the Senate, despite a veto by President Woodrow Wilson, and on January 17, 1920, Prohibition came into effect, making it illegal to manufacture, sell, or transport intoxicating liquors (above 4.5 percent ABV), with a few exceptions, such as alcohol used for medicinal purposes or ceremonial wine for Mass.

Although Prohibition was referred to as the Volstead Act, the most prominent author of this piece of legislation was Wayne Wheeler, a Prohibitionist from Ohio who had been lobbying to make America dry since 1893.

Left: Wayne Wheeler. *Right:* Andrew Volstead.

179. What Were the Consequences of Prohibition?

Although President Herbert Hoover would dub Prohibition the "noble experiment," its laws were consistently and purposefully ignored, culminating in a violent, deadly crime wave of unseen proportions that claimed thousands of lives.

Average Americans who wanted to enjoy an alcoholic beverage sometimes suffered health hazards from drinking illegally distilled bathtub gin called "rotgut," which was manufactured in thousands of households with materials that were available but harmful to humans, like cleaning products or varnish. Tobacco and iodine were used as

Al Capone

coloring agents to make the drink look more authentic. On the streets, wars were fought between the police and gangsters such as Al Capone over large quantities of smuggled whiskey. Not only were many civilians shot or murdered, but the repercussions on the American whiskey industry—which was almost completely destroyed—and the economy as a whole were grave. By the time Prohibition laws were repealed in 1933, the vast majority of distilleries had closed down for good.

"ALL I EVER DID WAS SUPPLY A DEMAND THAT WAS PRETTY POPULAR."

Al Capone

180. **What Role Did the Christian Temperance Movement Play in Prohibition?**

The seed of Prohibition was planted fifty years earlier by the Women's Christian Temperance Union (WCTU) and its determined president, Frances Willard. In 1874 they initiated the first temperance wave in the United States, during which large groups of women took to the streets in organized demonstrations, holding saloons under siege by singing psalms and reading proclamation texts against the "demon alcohol." Their efforts were certainly not unwarranted, what with many a sad example of alcoholism on the rise and men sometimes spending their entire week's wages on liquor instead of food for their families. As a result, women and children experienced starvation, poor living conditions, and physical abuse.

Frances Willard

Frances Willard was born in Churchville, New York, in 1839. She moved with her family to Wisconsin, where at age ten she made a solemn pledge with her older sister: "To quench our thirst we'll always bring Cold / water from the well or spring; / So here we pledge perpetual hate / To all that can intoxicate."

At its core, Willard's approach was a peaceful one, but the same cannot be said of Carry Amelia Moore, one of her most fanatical disciples. Carry (sometimes spelled Carrie) was born in Kentucky, the heartland of bourbon, in 1846. After an unfortunate marriage to a physician and alcoholic named Charles Gloyd, who managed to drink himself to death a mere month after the wedding, Carry left for Kansas. There she met and married David Nation, a lawyer. Her new name would become a source of dread for many publicans. Carry Nation wasn't peacefully spreading the Gospel; she was on a crusade of religious fundamentalism. She took on the Devil himself and was, by her own account, speaking to God, Jesus, the Holy Spirit, and a number of the disciples. Her opinion of men was harsh and to the point: "Men are nicotine-soaked, beer-besmirched, whiskey-greased, red-eyed devils."

In 1899, Carry Nation directed her first-ever attack, on the saloon of Mort Strong, in her hometown, Medicine Lodge, Kansas. Strong honored his name and threw her out of his establishment without flinching. But only a few weeks later, as a direct consequence of her tirades, four of the six saloons in town were closed. Carry Nation was bolstered by the steadily growing power of the temperance movement—a wave sweeping the United States, Canada, and Europe, especially Scotland, England, and Ireland. In February 1900, Carry's crusade became more aggressive, and she demolished a pharmacy with a sledgehammer, solely because it was selling

Carry Nation

brandy. In a 1901 raid, she used a small hatchet, a tool that would become her trademark. Her circle of power grew, and she continued on her mission, traveling as far as California and New York. She was gathering a large following of disciples fueled by her fiery speeches, until she died of a stroke on June 9, 1911.

181. Public Figures Supporting Prohibition

Religious zeal wasn't the only inspiration for Prohibition; the cause also had its proponents in the public and political sphere. William Jennings Bryan, a politician who had been appointed secretary of state in the Woodrow Wilson administration in the early twentieth century, was one of the most prominent political figures to join the cause. He'd accepted his posting on one condition—that he would not be obliged to serve alcoholic drinks during state dinners, choosing to offer the guests water and grape juice instead.

William Jennings Bryan

Originally, Bryan advocated free choice for every state regarding Prohibition, but with time he became convinced that the only solution was a nationwide ban of alcohol. For thirty years he was one of the most popular speakers in the nation addressing the topic of abstinence, and he traveled extensively. He focused his anti-alcohol preaching on rural areas: the Corn Belt, the Cotton Belt, and the Tobacco Belt. In these areas, his message against "demon alcohol" found fertile soil. During a thirty-day tour, he managed to raise a staggering $400,000 for the Anti-Saloon League, pocketing $11,000 to pay for his travel expenses.

When the Volstead Act became law in 1920, however, Bryan was reduced to a marginal figure, standing on the sidelines, watching his country deteriorate in an orgy of booze, corruption, and crime. Dying from cardiac arrest in 1925, he did not live to see its repeal.

At the turn of the twentieth century, Billy Sunday, a successful baseball player and converted Christian, committed himself to the same cause and stuck to it for decades to come. A true showman, he spoke the language of common folk, and one of his oft-repeated one-liners was "I'm going to knock John Barleycorn out of the box."

On January 16, 1920, just days before the National Prohibition Act came into effect, Billy Sunday performed his last act—a mock funeral for "John Barleycorn."

Billy Sunday

The boxing world had its own alcohol-banning booster too. In 1892, John L. Sullivan, the Boston Strong Boy, lost the heavyweight title to James J. Corbett. At first he sought solace in heavy drinking, but he soon repented and converted to Christianity. The temperance movement immediately presented him as an example of someone whose life was almost ruined by alcohol.

182. The Rise of Organized Crime During Prohibition

After William Jennings Bryan's death, the dark side of Prohibition began to reveal itself. Gangs of murderers and thugs used unheard-of cruelty to fight one another, and police officers were regularly bribed to look the other way while illegal beverages were trafficked into cities. The Scots happily accepted the necessary smuggling practices, exporting whisky to not only Canada but also the Bahamas, from where it would find its way into the United States.

Private clubs and speakeasies blossomed like never before. Officially the entire country was dry, but government officials would regularly find illegal pot stills in rural areas, as well as barrels full of whisky, which were destroyed on the spot. Unofficially, the United States was wetter than ever. A large speakeasy would easily make an annual profit of $500,000 in alcoholic beverages, and not one red cent would go into the national treasury. This was another effect of Prohibition: the national deficit grew quickly, caused in part by not collecting taxes on alcohol. A rough estimate at the time showed the federal government's annual loss at $50,000,000. Financially and morally, the "noble experiment" was heading for disaster.

Gangsters like Al Capone, Bugs Moran, Johnny Torrio, Hymie Weiss, and Dion O'Banion were the ones profiting most from the status quo. They weren't afraid of armed confrontations with one another, a turf war over illegal booze trade, and as a consequence, the streets of American cities from New York to New Orleans were soaked with blood. One of the worst incidents took place on Valentine's Day 1929 in Chicago, when seven members of Bugs Moran's gang were killed by Capone's cronies in an abandoned warehouse.

The public was in a state of shock over the supposed involvement of police officers in booze gang wars. The so-called St. Valentine's Day Massacre was a turning point. Neither civilians nor the police would stand for the ongoing violence fueled by the illegal alcohol trade any longer, and in Chicago more than 250 additional police detectives were hired. However, since Capone had used hired assassins from other parts of the country, it was extremely difficult to track them all down.

In the end, Capone was never convicted for the murders or smuggling whiskey, but was eventually found guilty of tax fraud. In 1931 America's most notorious gangster was sentenced to eleven years in prison. Eight years later he was released, but by that time he was an ill and broken man. When he eventually died in Florida in 1947, he was as poor as a church mouse. The man who claimed responsibility for catching Al Capone was federal agent Eliot Ness, who inspired a character on the TV series *The Untouchables*.

183. **The Real McCoy**

The most famous smuggler during Prohibition was Captain Bill McCoy, known for his excellent contraband, especially Cutty Sark whisky (see entry 136). His name eventually became synonymous with top-quality whiskey, and people started asking for "the Real McCoy" when they wanted uncut whiskey. When Prohibition was repealed in 1933, the brand already had a reputation in the United States and rapidly acquired more market share based on its success. Cutty Sark was the first Scotch whisky brand in America to sell more than 1 million 9-liter cases annually. McCoy's name is forever linked to this smooth-sippin' whisky.

184. **Repeal**

The end of Prohibition came when President Franklin D. Roosevelt proposed emergency measures to Congress. The 1929 Wall Street Crash and the subsequent Great Depression had depleted the government's finances, as well as those of its citizens, and brought about a general decline in morale. The president's New Deal presented a series of measures to help revive the failing economy. One of these measures was the repeal of Prohibition, which took place with the ratification of the Twenty-First Amendment on December 5, 1933. That same month, the Distilled Spirits Institute was founded in New York City. In 1973 it was renamed the Distilled Spirits Council of the United States (DISCUS).

185. The Aftermath of Prohibition

Schenley Products Company would play an important role in the resurrection of American alcoholic beverage production, distribution, and sales. An entirely new whiskey industry had to be built on the ruins of the "noble experiment." Only a handful of producers came to the fore, and they salvaged what they could—a single distillery, a stock of barrels that had escaped the government's attention, and many famous brand names that were revived by the new distilling elite. This is one of the reasons why, today, Heaven Hill Distillery in Louisville, Kentucky, has more than a hundred different brands on the market.

President Roosevelt also created the Federal Alcohol Control Administration (FACA), which was to write a code of conduct for the distilling industry. Eventually FACA would evolve into the Bureau of Alcohol, Tobacco, and Firearms. At first, each state was allowed to define its own rules regarding the production and sale of alcoholic beverages, which led to myriad laws that frequently contradicted one another. For example, one state would specify that liquor could be sold only with food, while another state would forbid that.

Over time, state laws have become more or less standardized, but imposing one national law is virtually impossible. Today, the sale of alcohol in some states is under a state monopoly, while in other states, liquor stores are private enterprises. To organize whiskey tastings in Seattle, Washington, one has to obtain a permit; whereas in Charleston, South Carolina, a restaurant owner can organize it himself, as long as he has a liquor license. Distillers have to jump through many hoops to register a new product nationwide; due to the multitude of laws among the different states, they usually need at least twenty-seven different labels.

CANADIAN WHISKY

186. How Is Canadian Whisky Made?

The Canadian way of distilling whisky is a complicated process. Virtually all Canadian whisky is blended whisky. But leaving it at that wouldn't do Canadians justice—their blending and fermentation techniques have developed into something of an art form. Here are four interesting aspects of their process:

1. Single Distillery

Canadian distillers do not swap casks like the Scots do, nor do they buy one another's products. Although each of the eight large distilleries produces various styles, each Canadian whisky is a "single distillery whisky." Canadian craftsmen don't use a mash bill like their American counterparts; they mill, mash, ferment, distill, and mature each grain distillate separately, only to blend them when fully matured. There are exceptions to the rule, however, like Canadian Club and Black Velvet, who blend their distillates before maturation.

2. Two Streams of Whisky

Regardless of the type of grain used, Canadian distillers create two different whisky streams that meet only after cask maturation—similar to a Scotch blend—but all parity ends there. The first stream is called "base whisky" and contains a very high level of alcohol (95 percent), but is low in congeners, which means it's pretty neutral in flavor. It will pick up most of its flavor from wooden casks during maturation.

Base whisky usually matures in casks previously used and forms the "elegant" part of Canadian whisky.

The second stream is called "flavoring whisky," distilled with a lower alcohol percentage from rye, wheat, barley, and/or corn. Maturation takes place in new oak casks or in a mix of new and used ones. Each flavoring whisky requires its own distilling regimen. Cask types, charring grades, and maturation times play an important role in the process.

Water from the Canadian Rockies makes its way to the distilleries.

3. **Flavor Additives**

It is permissible by law to add non-whisky-related flavoring agents to Canadian whisky following the so-called "9.09 percent" rule, meaning that a maximum of 9.09 percent of the bottled product can be a flavoring agent. The rule is more of a footnote in the entire production process, contrary to what online forums and bloggers would have us believe. However, imported Canadian whisky is also influenced by the American tax legislature. Whiskey producers in the United States get a tax break on

blends that add American-made whiskey to imported Canadian whisky, which means that certain brands of Canadian whisky may contain a flavoring additive in the United States, whereas they normally wouldn't in Canada. It's even more confusing that *wine* and *sherry* are words often used to describe the additives but the actual added liquid has nothing to do with those drinks. Last but not least, such additives have to mature in wooden casks before they can become part of a Canadian whisky.

4. Single Malts and Craft Distilling

Craft distilling is becoming as popular in Canada as it is in the United States and Europe. Currently there are more than thirty small craft distilleries in existence in Canada (some of them are shown on the map on page 297). An example of a single malt from Canada is Glen Breton, produced by a small distillery called Glenora, located in Nova Scotia.

Opposite, above: Empty casks at Valleyfield Distillery in Quebec, Canada, waiting to be filled with new make spirit. *Opposite, below:* Crown Royal is the showcase among Canadian whiskies. *Above:* In Nova Scotia, the Glenora Distillery produces single malt whisky.

187. What Is the Definition of Canadian Whisky?

Canadian whisky defies one description, because distilling varies by location and there isn't such a thing as a general Canadian law regarding whisky distilling. One can find a basic definition of Canadian whisky in the national Food and Drugs Act, but that cannot be considered the only set of rules and regulations in Canada. Somewhat paraphrased, this is the definition of Canadian whisky, Canadian rye whisky, or rye whisky:

A. ◆ Shall be a potable alcoholic distillate or a mixture of such distillates, made from a mash of grains or grain products, saccharified by the diastase of malt or any other enzymes, and fermented by yeast or a mixture of yeast and other microorganisms;

◆ Shall be matured in "small wood" during at least three years;

◆ Shall be a drink containing the aromas, flavors, and character in general credited to Canadian whisky;

◆ Shall be manufactured in line with tax laws and other applicable regulations;

◆ Shall be mashed, distilled, and matured in Canada and contain at least 40 percent ABV.

B. ◆ May contain caramel and other flavoring agents.

188. How Long Does Canadian Whisky Mature?

Canada was the first country in the world to define a minimum age for maturation: three years. The rule was created twenty-seven years before a similar rule was created in Scotland.

Gimli Distillery in Manitoba, Canada.

JAPANESE WHISKY

189. How Is Japanese Whisky Made?

In the beginning, Japanese distillers made only blended whisky, consisting of a domestic grain distillate mixed with single malt and blended whiskies imported from Scotland. Although the distilling process is similar, Japanese whisky has an entirely different flavor than Scottish single malts. Japanese whisky is even lighter, and distinguishes itself with a clarity of aromas. The absence of a grainy background is another difference from Scotch whisky, as is the use of the intensely aromatic Japanese oak for maturation.

Whisky writer Dave Broom described this in his *World Atlas of Whisky*: "If Scottish single malt is a rushing mountain burn, with all the flavours jostling for position, Japanese malt is a limpid pool where all is revealed."

Fermentation differs slightly too. The Japanese use a method called parallel dual fermentation—adding distillers' yeast and *koji*, a type of fungus used in East Asian cuisines to ferment soybeans, among other things. *Koji* comes in three varieties: *shiro koji-kin* (white fungus), *kuro koji-kin* (black fungus), and *ki koji-kin* (yellow fungus). They are used interchangeably, according to the distiller's preference. The use of *koji* is not allowed in European distilleries, which gives Japanese whisky a very unique character.

Opposite: Nikka is made and matured at Yoichi Distillery in Hokkaido, Northern Japan.

One of three mountain streams in the Japanese Alps that bring water to the
Hakushu Distillery.

190. How Long Does Japanese Whisky Mature?

Japanese whisky makers use second fill bourbon barrels and sherry casks or casks made of the indigenous mizunara oak. The array of Japanese single malts is broad because distillates from differently shaped stills are combined after maturation. The shape of a still influences the eventual taste of the whisky. This has to do with reflux (see entry 70), the amount of copper surface to which the distillate is exposed, the length of the swan neck, the angle of the lyne arm, and the condensation vessel used (see entry 73).

In the southern part of Japan, whisky usually matures at a more rapid pace than in the colder north, but the legal minimum is three years in the cask. Japan currently has eleven distilleries dispersed all over the country. Yamazaki, part of Suntory, is the largest and most famous among them. The map on page 299 shows their locations.

CHAPTER 4

IN THE BOTTLE AND ON THE BOTTLE

191. **When Is Whisky Bottled?**

The master blender decides when it's time to bottle the maturing whisky. He monitors the casks continually and has a huge array of samples at his disposal. Sometimes the marketing department requires a particular flavor profile. The master blender will then conduct a specific search in his liquid library and create a sample for a tasting panel. When the panel agrees, the casks related to the sample will be emptied and the contents blended and bottled. Whisky is always bottled after the minimum maturation time required by the country in which it is produced.

192. **Where Is Whisky Bottled?**

Most whisky is bottled in central bottling plants that work for various distilleries. In Scotland, a couple of distilleries have their own bottling facility, notably Bruichladdich, Springbank, Glen Grant, and Glenfiddich (which bottles only a small portion of the output on-site). In the United States, it is more common for distilleries to own and operate their bottling lines, which is the case with Jim Beam, Four Roses, and Jack Daniel's.

193. **What Is the Alcohol Percentage of Whisky at Bottling?**

The most common ABV percentages at bottling are 40 percent (the lowest permissible percentage for bottled whisky) and 43 percent. Each distiller has a preference, as do independent bottlers. In Scotland, most whisky is diluted to 63.5 percent ABV before it goes into the cask, and approximately 2 percent evaporates annually during maturation.

Opposite: A central bottling plant near Glasgow, Scotland.

194. **Is Whisky Diluted Before Bottling?**

Most whisky is diluted with demineralized water before bottling to achieve the desired ABV. Some whiskies are bottled undiluted, usually by independent bottlers. In such cases the label will state "cask strength" or "barrel strength."

195. **Is Whisky Filtered Before Bottling?**

Whisky is usually chill filtered before being bottled. This is done by lowering the temperature of the liquid below 39.2° Fahrenheit (4° Celsius). Various parts solidify in the process, and the filtering removes these undesired fatty acids and other impurities (like minuscule particles of charcoal from the cask). If a whisky is not chill filtered, the label will say "non-chill filtered." When mixed with water, or at colder temperatures, unfiltered whisky can turn cloudy. This is a natural and harmless occurrence.

196. Is Whisky Colored Before Bottling?

Coloring whisky with a minuscule amount of caramel (see entry 208) to retain color consistency is permissible by law. The amount of coloring additive is so tiny that it cannot be tasted. Still, laws in some European countries, like Sweden and Germany, mandate putting a disclaimer on the label (Germany uses the expression "mit Farbstoff"). In other countries this labeling isn't mandatory yet.

197. What Is Raw Cask Whisky?

Unfiltered whisky is called raw cask whisky. Small particles of charcoal may be floating in the bottle, so it's advisable to use a small strainer to remove these before consuming the whisky. Independent bottler Blackadder sells this type of whisky.

198. How to Read a Whisky Label

Think of the label as a passport to your whisky of choice. It provides a lot, if not all, of the information about the contents of the bottle.

- **ORIGIN.** Origin includes the country of production. The first indication of the type of whisky you're dealing with.

- **TYPE.** Type is a further classification: Kentucky straight bourbon, single malt, blended, etc. (See entry 200.)

- **REGION.** Region is a classification used predominantly for Scottish single malts, indicating where the whisky was produced: Speyside, Islay, Highlands, Campbeltown, Lowlands. This specification will sometimes be an indication of the flavor, but not always. Generally,

Islay malts are sturdy and smoky, the Lowlanders are light and delicate, and the other regions produce a spectrum of whiskies in between. Some exceptions are non-smoky whiskies made on Islay, and among Speyside whiskies—known for their fruity and flowery notes—an occasional peaty expression may appear.

- **AGE STATEMENT.** Age refers to the number of years the whisky has spent in the cask before being bottled. When a label designates whisky age, it always pertains to the youngest whisky in the bottle. Labels on American and Canadian whiskies usually don't provide age statements, but standard Scottish malts and premium blends often do. Some Scottish single malts provide two different age statements: the year of distillation and the year of bottling. These expressions are called vintage malt whiskies.

- **NAME.** Whiskies can be named for their distillery, but they can also carry an additional name, like The Macallan Amber, Talisker Storm, Aberlour A'Bunadh, Jim Beam Black, Jack Daniel's No. 27 Gold, and Wild Turkey Forgiven. These names may be a reference to a particular color, taste, maturation, surrounding, climate condition, or origin. Finally, a tailor-made whisky brand can also be named by the customer who ordered it.

- **DISTILLERY NAME.** In most cases, the name of the distillery is the same as its whisky. But there are always exceptions. Heaven Hill produces more than a hundred bourbon and rye whiskeys for their own brands and for third parties—only one of them carries the name of the distiller. Tobermory on the Isle of Mull produces an eponymous single malt and one called Ledaig.

- **ALCOHOL PERCENTAGE (ABV).** The alcoholic level at which the whisky was bottled is the ABV. Most whisky is diluted to 40 to 43 percent ABV before bottling. Undiluted whisky may contain more than 60 percent ABV. In that case, the label will provide the exact percentage and say "cask strength." American

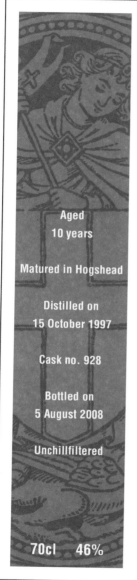

Aged
10 years

Matured in Hogshead

Distilled on
15 October 1997

Cask no. 928

Bottled on
5 August 2008

Unchillfiltered

70cl   46%

Speyside Single Malt Scotch Whisky

Distilled at Macallan Distillery
Vintage 1997

Cask individually selected
by Hans Offringa
for the

City of Zwolle

Bottle no. *1* of 350

Bottled by Signatory Vintage Scotch Whisky Co. Ltd.
Pitlochry PH16 5JP Scotland
Label design by Gijs Dragt

whiskeys often include "proof" on the label. Rule of thumb: divide proof by two and you'll know the ABV (for example, 90 proof is 45 percent ABV).

- **FILTERING.** Most whiskies are chill filtered prior to bottling, to remove any impurities. Some are not filtered, in which case the label will say "un-chill filtered" or "non-chill filtered."

- **VOLUME.** A standard bottle in the United States will hold 75 cl, whereas 70 cl is more common in Europe. Various brands also bottle at 20 cl, 35 cl, 1 liter, and 1.75 liter. Miniatures normally contain 5 cl.

- **FOUNDATION DATE.** When mentioned on an official distillery bottling, it is the date when the distillery was founded. When mentioned on an independent bottling, it refers to the date when the bottling company was founded.

- **BOTTLING COMPANY NAME.** By law it is mandatory to state on the label the name of the company that bought and bottled the whisky.

- **LOGO.** The visual identity of the whisky is shown in the form of a logo. Some very famous logos have undergone updates over the years. The striding man on Johnnie Walker bottles used to walk from right to left; today he is walking in the other direction. Gilbert the Grouse of The Famous Grouse label used to wear a meticulously drawn feathered suit; his current attire resembles a tux.

- **TASTING NOTE.** The tasting note is not always included with a bottle of whisky. If you can't find it on the label, you might see it on the back label of the bottle or packaging. When the whisky is packaged in a tube, a small booklet with brand information and a tasting note may accompany the bottle inside. Laphroaig often includes this kind of booklet in order to promote its loyalty program, the Friends of Laphroaig.

199. What Does the Origin Tell Me?

The origin is an indication of the country where the whisky was distilled and matured. The grain used to make whisky may come from anywhere in the world. Scotland has a rule that the whisky also has to be bottled in the country itself; other countries are less specific. Lots of American whiskey is exported to Europe in bulk and bottled at local bottling plants.

200. What Does the Type Tell Me?

The type tells you which grains were used to make the whisky and sometimes even where the whisky comes from. Single malt, for example, can be made of only malted barley but can be distilled anywhere. Japanese whisky clearly comes from Japan but can be blended with Scotch. Bourbon always has to come from the United States, and so on.

201. What Does the Age Tell Me?

The age on the label tells you how much time the whisky spent in a cask. Contrary to popular belief, older whiskies aren't always better than younger ones. A whisky that spends too much time in the wood can turn into "oak juice"—a bitter liquid with a tannic aftertaste. On the other hand, too little time spent maturing in a cask may cause the whisky to taste raw and unbalanced.

202. **Are Age Statements Mandatory?**

In Scotland, Ireland, Japan, and Canada an age statement is not mandatory. In the United States, an age statement is obligatory only when the whiskey inside the bottle is younger than four years and is applicable only to straight whiskeys. The rest of the whiskey world operates without mandatory age information.

203. **What Does the Name Tell Me?**

The name on the bottle does not necessarily provide reliable information on the whisky's origin. Glen Breton, for instance, is a Canadian single malt and not a Scottish one, as one might expect given the fact that the word *glen* is used almost exclusively for Scotch whisky. However, the label will indicate the country of origin.

204. **What Does *ABV* Mean?**

ABV is an abbreviation for "alcohol by volume." Depending on the country where the whisky is sold, the alcohol content may be expressed simply as a percentage on the label without including *ABV*. Whisky has to contain at least 40 percent ABV, or be 80 proof, to be called whisky.

205. **What Is the Volume of a Whisky Bottle?**

Amounts in the bottle vary per country (see page 176). There is no legal standard defined. In Europe most whisky is bottled at 70 cl; in the United States it's 75 cl.

206. **What Does *Proof* Mean?**

The word *proof* originated in eighteenth-century England, as a measure for the percentage of alcohol in a beverage. Proof was tested by setting fire to the distillate with the aid of gunpowder. A solution of alcohol and water "proved" itself when the mixture caught fire. If not, it was called underproof. At that time, 100 proof equaled 57.15 percent ABV.

This measurement is no longer used in Europe. The United States has its own "proof," which is twice the ABV stated. Some labels will express the alcohol content both ways.

207. What Does *NAS* Mean?

NAS stands for "No Age Statement." These are whiskies without any age information. The term was invented by consumers, not by producers.

208. What Is E150a?

E150a is a caramel coloring agent permitted in whisky in tiny quantities to secure the color consistency of the end product. Caramel does not affect the taste; it is purely cosmetic.

209. What Does *Single Malt* Mean?

Single malt whisky is made from malted barley only, at one single distillery, in copper pot stills.

210. What Is an Independent Bottler?

The first commercial brokers appeared on the scene in the nineteenth century, and they are the predecessors of present-day independent bottlers. They were merchants who bought whisky casks in bulk at various distilleries. They either blended and bottled the contents or sold entire casks to pubs, bars, restaurants, and the occasional wealthy individual.

Casks that are purchased by bottlers often have to stay at the distillery itself, either because of logistics or lack of space. However, the bottler has free rein over the purchased stock and decides when the contents

should be bottled. The master distiller of the respective distillery has no say in that. Some big international independent bottlers are Adelphi, Cadenhead, Duncan Taylor, Douglas Laing, Gordon & MacPhail, Morrison & Mackay, and Signatory.

211. What Is the Difference Between an Official Distillery Bottling and an Independent One?

Official bottlings are always launched by the owner of the whisky brand; independent bottlings are not. The whisky bottled by independent bottlers may be labeled with a different name than the one the distillery uses, and some distilleries don't even allow independent bottlings of their stock to carry the distillery name (prompting one independent bottler to name its product "The One That Cannot Be Named"). A difference may be noticed in the alcohol by volume (ABV) as well.

212. What Is a Single Cask or Single Barrel Bottling?

When the label states *single cask* or *single barrel* it means the whisky is bottled from only one cask or barrel. The quantity of bottles is limited, and often each bottle is numbered (for example "No. 56 of 342 bottles").

213. What Is a Limited Edition?

Limited-edition whiskies are launched in limited quantities at a given time. They don't necessarily need to be a single cask or single barrel whisky. In the United States, the term *small batch* is used as an equivalent. Distillers will sometimes launch a specific series of limited bottlings, such as the Valhalla Collection of Highland Park, which consisted of Thor, Loki, Freya, and Odin.

214. **What Types of Bottles Are Used?**

Glass is the most common material for whisky bottles, but plastic is used too, especially in the United States, where plastic is praised as "the unbreakable bottle." The standard volume of the bottle is 75 cl in the United States, whereas most European countries use 70 cl bottles. One-liter bottles are usually intended only for duty-free shops, but sometimes they appear in local liquor stores. This is due to a practice known as "parallel import," which occurs when wholesalers use loopholes to purchase outside standard import regulations. There is a standard shape for whisky bottles, but most distilleries prefer to come up with a unique design for their products to distinguish themselves from competitors.

Left: A standard bottle as used by GlenDronach single malt whisky. *Right:* A specially designed bottle for Cardhu single malt whisky.

215. How Long Can I Keep Whisky?

Whisky in the cask can be kept for years, provided it does not go below 40 percent ABV (no longer legally whisky) or evaporate entirely. Bottled whisky has an unlimited life span, as long as no oxygen can get to the liquid. Once the bottle is opened, the whisky slowly oxidizes and could become bland, or the character may change. The smaller the amount of whisky left in the bottle, the more rapid the deterioration. Rule of thumb: finish a bottle within two to three years of opening it if you want to drink the whisky at its best. Whisky, unlike other comestibles, cannot go bad.

216. What Is the Best Method for Storing Whisky?

The ideal conditions for keeping your whisky safe and retaining its quality is to store it at room or cellar temperature. Some whisky that is kept in cold conditions may turn cloudy. Elements in the liquid will coagulate, but it won't affect the taste. It is advisable to keep the bottle out of direct sunlight in an upright position, occasionally turning the bottle upside down to dampen the cork. Laying the bottle down may cause the glue that attaches the cork to the stopper to dissolve from contact with alcohol, which will definitely make your whisky go sour.

217. What Happens to Whisky in the Bottle?

Contrary to wine, whisky does not mature further in the bottle. As long as the cork or screw cap closes the bottle hermetically, nothing really happens to it. Once the bottle has been opened, oxidation will have its effect on the whisky and the taste will slowly deteriorate. The whisky won't go bad; it will just lose its original character. The higher the ABV content, the slower the rate of deterioration. To keep the taste, you may seal an opened bottle with paraffin, or vacuum the air out of the bottle with the aid of a Vacu Vin, a small pump originally designed for open wine bottles.

218. What Is the Old Bottle Effect?

The so-called old bottle effect (OBE) is a topic of discussion among whisky aficionados. Some believe that whisky kept in an unopened bottle for a very long time slowly changes tastewise. However, this remains a matter of debate. When an old bottle is opened, the whisky is suddenly exposed to oxygen, which might change its flavor. It wouldn't be unreasonable to assume that whisky made thirty to forty years ago tastes different from today's whisky to begin with—if we compared whiskies from the same brands today with those from thirty years ago, some will have changed drastically in character, while others hardly at all.

If the fill level seems significantly lower than that of a new bottle, it means the old bottle hasn't been closed properly, and oxidation will take its toll in such a case. However, there is no scientific evidence for OBE. The only clear difference in bottles is that they were not coated on the inside until the 1970s. Whether such a coating could contribute to the taste remains a question.

219. When Is a Screw Cap Used?

There are no guidelines on screw caps—it is up to the preference of the distiller. Many whiskies are bottled with a screw cap, even old bottlings such as Gordon & MacPhail's Connoisseurs Choice range. When applied tightly, it is an excellent way to seal off a bottle.

Teacher's was the first whisky marketed with a screw cap, in 1913.

220. **When Is a Cork Used?**

When a descendant of the Teacher family invented the screw cap in 1913, the usage of cork gradually declined but managed to make a comeback several decades ago. Single malt whiskies and the more expensive varieties are usually corked. It is advisable to turn an unopened bottle upside down regularly to keep the cork moist. A "corked" whisky (whisky contaminated by cork taint) is rare.

221. **Why Do So Many Scottish Whisky Names Begin with *Glen*?**

In the old days, when distilling whisky in the Scottish Highlands was mostly done illegally, due to the fact that licenses were very expensive, distillers had to hide their equipment from English Customs and Excise officers on the lookout for perpetrators. *Glen* is a Scottish word for valley, and due to its topographical characteristics, it is a prime location for camouflaging a hidden pot still. In addition, rivers or streams usually run through glens, and plenty of water is vital to making whisky. *Strath*, which is a broader valley than a glen, is another word that shows up in brand names like Strathmill and Strathisla. One of the most famous glens in Scotland is the glen of the River Livet.

Opposite: Cork stoppers ready for use on a bottling line at Jim Beam in Clermont, Kentucky. *Following pages:* The Glenlivet Distillery, nestled in the glen of the River Livet, produces one of the world's best-known single malts.

CHAPTER 5

TASTING
WHISKY

222. What Kind of Glass Should I Use to Drink Whisky?

Nosing and tasting start with the choice of the perfect drinking vessel. The well-known broad tumbler glass makes drinking easy and is the suitable type of glass for whisky on the rocks. If you like mixing whisky with ginger ale, cola, or soda water, you may prefer a tall glass. But if you're looking for the finer nuances in flavor and aroma, you may want to try a special tasting glass: tapered on the top, rounded at the bottom. In this type of glass, sometimes referred to as tulip or copita, whisky can be well swirled, and the narrow opening prevents aromas from escaping too quickly. Such tasting glasses can be found in different shapes and sizes, with or without a stem. Some even have glass lids for further aroma preservation. Pour about an ounce into the glass, swirl the whisky slowly, and take the time to enjoy its color.

223. How Do I Nose Whisky?

Smell the whisky by keeping your nose about half an inch to an inch above the glass. Note the difference between nosing with your mouth closed and open. Take little sniffs like a rabbit, and breathe out through your mouth. A thorough sniff with your nose deep in the glass will cause the alcohol to anesthetize your olfactory receptors and you won't taste or smell much for the next ten to fifteen minutes.

224. How Do I Taste Whisky?

Observing, nosing, tasting, and experiencing the mouthfeel gives us a range of ways to experience and enhance the enjoyment of whisky. Tasting is an important part of this appreciation and deserves to be done slowly. Have a tiny sip. Don't swallow the liquid immediately but allow it to wash over each corner of your mouth. You will recognize sweet, salty, bitter, and sour flavors, not all of the same intensity. When you are not accustomed to strong liquor containing 40 percent ABV or more, you may want to take a sip of water first, then a sip of whisky—you'll detect flavors and aromas but avoid the burn of the alcohol.

225. How Many Flavors and Aromas Can Be Detected?

Experts have discovered and described hundreds of flavors and aromas, relatively easy to divide into ten main groups: flowers, fruits, malt, vanilla, smoke, wood, honey, nuts, spices, and medicinal. Most people recognize the first five. The next five require more training and experience. When you start to pick up aromas of fruit or flowers in your whisky, you will ascertain more nuances after a while and indeed recognize apple, pineapple, banana, or violets and jasmine too. Whisky writer Charles MacLean developed a Whisky Wheel—a practical tool for categorizing aromas (see following page).

All aromas you detect were created naturally, as whisky cannot legally have any additives to enhance flavor (with the exception of Canadian whisky) and still be called whisky. More than 60 percent of whisky's aromas and flavors are created by the type of cask the liquid matured in, combined with the maturation period, the location in the warehouse, and the ambient microclimate. Generally speaking, whisky from a European oak cask will have more aromas of dried fruit. Vanilla is typical for whiskies matured in American oak casks. A smoky aroma in a whisky is obtained by drying the malted barley over a peat fire. Peat itself has no smell, but its smoke contains certain particles called phenols, which attach themselves to the barley seeds. These minuscule particles eventually give such "peaty" whiskies as Ardbeg, Bowmore, Lagavulin, and Laphroaig their distinctive smoky flavors and aromas.

CHARLES MACLEAN'S
WHISKY WHEEL

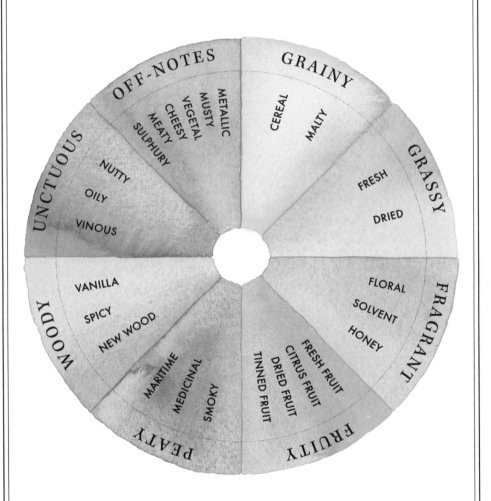

Naturally, some people are better at picking up aromas than others. Sometimes it's a matter of circumstance: if you recently suffered a cold or ate garlic or a spicy curry, your palate and nose are compromised. Is the whisky warm or cold? This has an influence on aromas rising from the glass. Apart from these circumstances, not everybody possesses the talent to describe clearly what he or she is tasting in a whisky. This is no reason for concern; taste is as individual as it gets. The most important part is whether you like the whisky or you don't.

226. What Is the Body of Whisky?

When you taste a few different whiskies, you will notice that some feel "thin" and others more oily, like a "fat" Chardonnay wine. This is called the body of whisky. It doesn't say anything about the quality. Keep your glass at a 45-degree angle, swirl it around for 360 degrees, right it again, and see the "tears" running down the bowl of the glass. The thinner and runnier the tear, the higher the percentage of alcohol; the slower the tear, the more complex and oily the whisky is.

227. What Is a Finish?

The finish, or aftertaste, of whisky may be short, long, heavy, quiet, or explosive. After swallowing the whisky, you will notice whether the taste lingers or quickly disappears.

228. What Is a Shot Glass?

The shot glass was made popular by many a Western movie. Its name first appears in a book from 1913, written by a Dr. Jehu Z. Powell, titled *History of Cass County Indiana: From Its Earliest Settlement to the Present Time*. A full whiskey barrel on a railway platform in New Waverly, Indiana, was ready to be picked up by a saloon owner. A fanatical proponent of total abstinence from drinking shot a hole in the barrel to empty the contents. The amber-red liquid poured out of the hole, and all the publican got was an empty barrel. Since then, the customers would ask for "a shot of red eye." Those who prefer to down a whiskey in one go will want to use this type of glass.

229. What Is a Highball?

The highball is a tall glass used mostly for cocktails. Its name has become synonymous with mixed drinks. Its origins, however, are not entirely clear: one source mentions the railroads, where the word *highball* was used for a signal that meant "clear track ahead."

"A GOOD GULP OF HOT WHISKEY
AT BEDTIME—IT'S NOT VERY
SCIENTIFIC, BUT IT HELPS."

Alexander Fleming

Opposite: Jack Daniel's presents a whole series of shot glasses, as well as a small tumbler and a highball.

230. What Is a Tumbler?

A tumbler is a wide, heavy glass shorter than a highball. The original design sported a pointy bottom, so the glass couldn't stand upright on its own and had to be emptied before it was put down. Many contemporary tumblers have a flat bottom, but try the following: place an empty tumbler on its side. If it rolls back into an upright position, it is the genuine product. This is the glass loved by those who prefer to drink their whisky on the rocks.

During the annual Kentucky Bourbon Festival cocktail gala, each distiller gives its signature tumbler to the attendees. You get an empty goody bag to carry all the tumblers you collect.

In the foreground, a series of tumblers; in the background, a series of nosing glasses.

231. **What Is a Nosing Glass or Snifter?**

Originally the nosing glass, or snifter, was a wide glass on a stem with a round tapered body, meant for the enjoyment of brandy or cognac. Its special design allows the liquid to breathe while the aromas assemble in the upper part of the glass. Various versions are available; the one used most often for whisky is the Glencairn glass, developed in 2001. The British manufacturing company that pioneered it received the Queen's Award for Enterprise in 2006. It is a sturdy type of glass, beloved among festival organizations and distillers alike, some of whom may choose to have their logo etched on. Distillery shops usually sell them for under $10.

The award-winning Glencairn glass.

232. **What Is a Quaich?**

Quaichs are Scottish shallow drinking cups or bowls with two flat handles. They come in wood, earthenware, glass, pewter, and silver, sometimes with a logo etched on the inside. Traditionally the quaich is used for ceremonial purposes.

233. **Do I Need to Decant Whisky?**

It is not necessary to decant whisky beforehand. It might look nice when it's being served, but decanting has more disadvantages than advantages. Old crystal decanters can release lead into your whisky, which is not good for your health. Moreover, the whisky's taste will subtly change as soon as it's exposed to oxygen. Various whiskies are sold in sealed decanters made of lead-free crystal or porcelain. The latter can be damaged after some time as the alcohol slowly erodes it.

234. What Is a Dram?

Dram is a term often used by the Scots for a glass of whisky. A "wee dram" literally means a small volume, but in practice the word is often used ironically, as the amount one is talking about is the exact opposite. The root of the word is the Greek *drachma*, which can be a coin or a weight. A "solid" dram weighs 1.77 grams and a "liquid" dram measures 35 ml in Great Britain. Many English pubs only pour 25 ml, whereas Scottish publicans tend to respect the 35 ml. A shot, the dram's equivalent in the United States, tends to be 1.5 fluid ounces, about 44 ml.

235. What Is the Effect of Adding Ice to Whisky?

Ice anesthetizes the palate. The colder the whisky, the less diversity in flavor and aroma can be detected. However, ice can also evoke unexpected thrills. Ice-cold whisky combined with a piece of chocolate, a bonbon, or a chocolate dessert provides a very pleasant sensation. The same goes for a whisky cocktail.

236. What Is the Effect of Adding Water to Whisky?

Adding water opens the whisky and reveals more aromas. But beware—too much of it can drown a whisky, and old whiskies may completely collapse. A plastic pipette is a handy tool for adding water by the drop. There's no golden rule; in the end, how much water to add is a matter of trial and error and personal preference.

237. What Is a Tasting Note?

A tasting note is a written description of a whisky's color, nose, taste, body, and finish. Official tasting notes may be found on the label or packaging of a whisky or a distillery's website, while tasting notes from whisky writers are more often found in books and magazines. Some whisky writers develop their own methods of arriving at numerical scores. Others prefer to write prosaic paragraphs to describe their impressions. Whisky often triggers a feeling or a memory of a certain place or event—this can often be read in such qualitative tasting notes.

238. How Do I Write My Own Tasting Notes?

First, describe the *color* (yellow, gold, bronze, or amber). Then, concentrate on the first impression your *nose* picks up, and use a broad category term like *flowers, fruit, smoke,* or *wood.* You can then take a small sip and describe the mouthfeel or *body.* It may be oily, thin, or dry. Note your first taste impression, again using a broad term: *fruit, flowers, grain,* etc. Finally, notice the finish when swallowing the whisky: short, medium-long, long, or lingering. Repeat the process and see if the second time around you can name the flavors and aromas somewhat more specifically. For example, with fruity flavors, you might be able to recognize pear, banana, or lychee; with flowery ones it might be jasmine, rose, or violet; with woody flavors it might be cedar, cigar box, or vanilla.

You can add a tiny splash or a few drops of water and repeat the previously described steps. The molecular structure of the liquid will change—the whisky will open up and release more aromas.

It takes time and practice to distinguish one whisky from another. Some people naturally detect aromas better than others. For those who find it difficult to describe the nose and taste, a descriptive comparison may come in handy: "This smells like my grandmother's spice cupboard" or "This smells like a recently doused campfire on the beach." Tasting whisky has an emotional component as well. Connecting an emotion to a certain experience will anchor a whisky or a distinctive flavor profile in your memory, and next time you will recognize that particular whisky faster. But, above all, taste is and always will be a personal experience.

239. What Are the Different Types of Tastings?

A tasting session, or simply tasting, offers a series of whiskies to taste. This can be done alone or with a group of friends (the latter being more fun, especially when comparing one another's experiences). Depending on your preferences, you can put together different types of tastings.

A horizontal tasting includes whiskies of one particular genre, for example, five different single malts from five different distilleries, or five different bourbons. A vertical tasting consists of vintages from one and the same distillery. Glenfarclas is an excellent choice for such a tasting. This Scottish whisky company not only has a standard series with different age statements, but it also releases the Family Casks reserve series, for those who want to try a whisky distilled in their birth year. Festivals are a good place to attend a tasting or get acquainted with a fair amount of readily available whiskies. Specialized whisky shops may offer tastings and will usually charge an admission fee.

240. How Do I Arrange a Tasting?

If you plan to taste a series of different whiskies side by side, pour all the glasses beforehand. It is advisable to drink a little water between whiskies or eat a small piece of dry bread. The use of ice is not forbidden, but the senses will be anesthetized and the whisky will be cooled, resulting in a more limited sensation when nosing and tasting. However, if you can't do without it, add ice. The most important thing is to drink the whisky as you enjoy it most. A useful side note for planning: approximately thirty-seven glasses can be poured from a 75 cl bottle of whisky when pouring a standard tasting amount (2 cl).

241. What Are the Dos and Don'ts of Pairing Food with Whisky?

Whisky and food can be wonderful together. You can choose harmonious or contrasting flavors when pairing them—both methods make the whole greater than the sum of its parts. An example of a harmonious pairing would be choosing foods with aromas and flavors similar to those found in a whisky, like a nutty cheese with Glen Garioch. You don't have to limit yourself to combining smoky whiskies with smoked food, however. Contrasting flavors are also interesting. Ardbeg, a smoky whisky, works well with a tasty chervil-spinach soup, scallops, or a strong Époisses, or in a citrus fruit salad. Single malts are most suitable for drinking with food due to their distinctive flavor profiles—and different foods can reveal the single malt's versatility.

Whisky may either be an accompaniment to the meal or added to it by injecting a small amount into a dish or by using the whisky in a marinade. The flambé technique is less suitable—it may look spectacular, but it burns off all the alcohol and, with it, the aromas and flavors.

242. Which Whiskies Go Well with Fish?

Clynelish, Glenmorangie, Oban, and Old Pulteney are good companions to fish. They add a sweet, briny note to the dish. A lobster or seafood bisque pairs beautifully with the whiskies from these four maritime distilleries. A few drops of Talisker on an oyster or sprayed onto a small piece of smoked salmon (using an atomizer) works well too. Young Speyside whiskies, especially those matured in ex-bourbon barrels, are good companions to a creamy sauce over fish.

243. Which Whiskies Go Well with Meat?

Glenfarclas fifteen-year-old whisky is delicious served with duck breast with orange sauce. Ex–sherry cask matured whiskies usually pair well with beef and game. A whiff of oak wood goes well with a spicy sauce or meat dishes with dried-fruit stuffing. Glenmorangie Nectar d'Or complements lamb tajine with apricots and almonds. Spareribs or warm ham slices with honey sauce feel at home with bourbon—look for a spicy one, such as Four Roses Single Barrel or Wild Turkey 101.

244. Which Whiskies Go Well with Vegetarian Dishes?

Expressions from both ex-bourbon barrels and ex-sherry casks can be considered for pairing with vegetables. Carrots, for example, have an earthy note, while grains emphasize the malty character of a whisky. A few examples of good combinations: Aberlour eighteen-year-old whisky with a wild mushroom risotto or Lagavulin sixteen-year-old whisky with celery root soup or toasted hazelnuts.

245. Which Whiskies Go Well with Cheese?

Each type of cheese demands its own whisky. So when serving a platter of various cheeses, you are in for a challenge. The following combinations have a proven track record: blue cheeses pair well with smoky malt whiskies; cheddar requires whiskies matured in ex-bourbon barrels, such as Auchentoshan or Glen Garioch; ripe cheeses, for instance a Comté, old Gouda, or Gruyère, go well with older fruity/malty single malts like The Macallan or GlenDronach.

246. Which Whiskies Go Well with Chocolate?

The darker the chocolate, the sturdier the whisky has to be. Look for distinctive wood notes like those in malts matured in ex-sherry casks. Dalmore twelve-year-old is a fine example, as are the older Glenfarclas expressions. Milk chocolate, pralines, and white chocolate are complemented by a creamier malt matured in ex-bourbon casks—think The Glenlivet Founders Reserve or the twelve-year-old version. Salted chocolate demands smoky whisky—the twelve-year-old Bowmore of Islay with a salted panna cotta fudge is a feast in itself.

The Macallan and chocolate are a match made in heaven.

247. Which Whiskies Go Well with Cigars?

Whisky and cigars can make a fine pair. One of the signature events of the Kentucky Bourbon Festival is an outdoor banquet at which visitors can enjoy the combination. The Dalmore Distillery in the Highlands of Scotland developed a special single malt called the Cigar Malt. Balvenie, sister distillery to Glenfiddich, launched a Caribbean Cask single malt, which spent extra time maturing in casks that previously held rum. Both single malts can stand their ground with a Cuban or Nicaraguan long filler. Bourbons such as Four Roses Single Barrel, Wild Turkey Rare Breed, or Jim Beam Double Oak all pair well with cigars. However, some of the more delicate whiskies can get lost when paired with a cigar—smoke can desensitize the nose and palate, causing subtle aromas and flavors to disappear.

248. How Many Glasses Can I Pour from a Bottle of Whisky?

You can pour about thirty-five glasses from a 70 cl bottle and about thirty-seven glasses from a 75 cl bottle. These estimates are based on 2 cl pours, which is a suitable amount for nosing and tasting.

249. What Are Some Especially Good Whisky Cocktails?

Some favorites include the Manhattan, the Old-Fashioned, and the Whiskey Sour. These cocktails are classics; they're predominantly made with bourbon or rye whiskey. In recent years, bartenders and mixologists have discovered that single malts are great for creating new cocktails, especially smoky ones. For example, the Penicillin, with a mean dash of Laphroaig, is a current favorite. But the trend isn't all that new—in the 1980s, famous tenor saxophonist Dexter Gordon used to ask for a smoky martini, demanding it be made with Lagavulin.

A cocktail with Highland Park twelve-year-old being prepared in Amsterdam's speakeasy Door 74.

250. Men's Versus Women's Whiskies

The lighter and sweeter whiskies in the spectrum, like Glengoyne, Dalwhinnie, Auchentoshan, Glen Grant, and The Glenlivet, are often seen as "women's whiskies." The sturdy, smoky ones and the serious sherry bombs are often referred to as belonging to the male domain. However, this is an artificial division that has been rebutted many times over. There are many women who love the smoky variety or heavily sherried expressions, as well as plenty of men going for the lighter whisky flavors.

251. How Can I Become a Whisky Connoisseur?

An amateur whisky lover can blossom into a real connoisseur by tasting many different whiskies and comparing their flavor profiles. However, this takes a lot of time, training, and money, as is the case with any hobby or profession you want to excel in. Those who cannot afford to invest in one or all three might find a shortcut in *The Bluffer's Guide to Whisky* by David Milsted, a book that is surprisingly accurate, albeit somewhat of a surface-level presentation of the subject matter. After reading it, you might be able to pass for a connoisseur at a party, until you find yourself face-to-face with a real authority.

252. How Do I Interpret Whisky Scores from Authors?

Various whisky writers use scoring methods when writing tasting notes. This can be a numerical score, as in *Jim Murray's Whisky Bible* and Michael Jackson's *Malt Whisky Companion*, but also with an intensity score, as applied in David Wishart's *Whisky Classified*. The scores are by definition subjective. Many writers refrain from giving numerical scores, preferring to describe the whiskies, then compare their own tasting experience with the intentions of the whisky makers. In the end, the only score that really matters is your own—and it may be quite different from the score of a professional whisky writer.

253. Whisky Clubs

Whisky clubs both large and small can be found all over the world. What was likely the first attempt to form a whisky club took place around 1978 in Scotland, when Phillip Hills, a world-renowned whisky expert and author of *Appreciating Whisky*, started buying casks directly from distilleries with a couple of friends. Soon enough, the Scotch Malt Whisky Society (SMWS) was born.

Today, some clubs have online forums and magazines; others organize monthly tastings. A membership is usually affordable and sometimes comes with discounts on whisky, offered by a liquor store in the region. Attending club meetings is an excellent way of getting better acquainted with the drink, by not only talking to seasoned members, but also conducting one's own "liquid research": sipping and sampling before buying a whole bottle. For more information on whisky clubs and organizations, see Resources (page 303).

Opposite: Tulip-shaped glasses are covered to retain aromas and flavors before a tasting session commences.

CHAPTER 6

BUYING
AND
INVESTING
IN
WHISKY

254. Why Is Whisky More Expensive Than Most Other Distillates?

Whisky usually matures longer than other distillates and is bottled at a minimum of 40 percent ABV. The higher percentage of alcohol and substantial maturation time contribute to a higher price, as does the fact that during maturation a portion of the contents of the cask will evaporate—the so-called angels' share (see entry 106).

255. What Defines the Worth of a Whisky?

The price of a bottle of whisky is defined by various factors: demand, availability, type, age, origin, percentage of alcohol (ABV), and number of bottles produced.

256. Where Can I Buy Whisky?

In some American states, whisky sales are restricted to state-run liquor stores. In other states, rules and regulations for selling liquor are less restrictive. Whisky sales are state-controlled in Sweden too, but not in the Netherlands, although you can't buy whisky at a supermarket there. In certain European countries, like Belgium and France, whisky is sold in supermarkets.

Opposite, above: A collection of exceptional whiskies at Scotch Whisky International (SWI). *Opposite, below:* Eric Bartels's famous shop in Zwolle, the whisky capital of the Netherlands.

257. **Can Whisky Be Sold Online?**

Various websites sell whisky, through either a virtual liquor store, a distillery webshop, or auctions. Legally speaking, it isn't always clear if online sales are aboveboard. Some countries allow the shipping of bottles containing a high ABV; others do not. If you plan to make an online purchase, carefully check the alcohol shipping regulations in your country beforehand, as well as the additional shipping costs that may apply.

258. **What Supermarkets Sell Whisky?**

Most supermarkets in the United States do not sell whisky, although grocery-store spirit sales of some kind are allowed in twenty-seven states. Supermarkets in many European countries—including Great Britain, France, Belgium, and Germany—do permit whisky sales.

259. **What About Whisky Auctions?**

Online auctions are either general or specialized. Catawiki, a European general auction website, sometimes offers whisky but does not specialize in it. Some dedicated online whisky auction sites include WhiskyAuction.com, Bonhams.com, Whisky-OnlineAuctions.com, ScotchWhiskyAuctions.com, WhiskyAuctioneer.com, and Just-Whisky.co.uk.

260. **How Can I Make a Bid Online?**

Most auction sites ask you to create a profile before you can put in a bid. It is also possible to sell whisky through these websites, but be prepared to give the auctioneer a generous cut of 15 to 20 percent.

261. How Can I Invest in Whisky?

As with most investments today, you can buy and sell whisky collections on the Internet without an intermediary. Those who seek professional guidance can contact Scotch Whisky International (SWI), a company based in the Netherlands. Unique in the industry, SWI creates whisky portfolios for prospective investors and houses collections for its customers.

262. How Can I Choose the Best Brand to Invest In?

Investing in whisky is similar to investing in stocks and bonds—it takes a bit of a gut feeling, a willingness to take a risk, and a close monitoring of market trends. One way to familiarize yourself with the market, for example, is by following online auctions. *Liquid Gold*, a book by Ralph L. Warth, is a useful guide. In this hefty tome, Warth has defined a set of objective criteria for investing in whisky and rates close to 18,000 different whiskies.

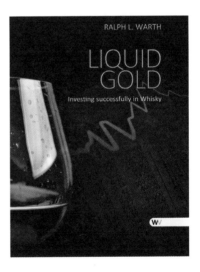

263. What to Sell and What to Keep?

Whiskies from the 1970s (because of their rarity, slightly different production methods, and perceived quality), whiskies from closed distilleries, and iconic brands like The Macallan are usually sound investments and worth keeping. So are special limited editions in stylish packaging. A fine example is the Highland Park fifty-year-old in a sterling silver casing designed by Maeve Gillies, a jewelry designer born on Orkney and currently living in New York.

Once in a while, pre-Prohibition whiskey will appear on the market. Its value lies in its scarcity as much as in the fact that it's a historical souvenir, which is why some might choose to taste it while others might want to keep the bottles intact. Again, watch the auctions to get a feel for when to buy and when to sell.

264. What Is the Best Way to Store an Unopened Bottle of Whisky?

Unopened bottles of whisky are best kept at room temperature, in an upright position, out of direct sunlight. A cellar is a good storage place, as long as the temperature is not too low. Some parts of whisky start solidifying, and the whisky can get cloudy at temperatures below 41° Fahrenheit (5° Celsius). But the cloudiness only changes the appearance; it does not influence the quality and taste. If a bottle has been standing in an upright position for a long time, turn it upside down once in a while to moisten the cork. Otherwise the cork might break into little pieces when the bottle is opened.

265. What Are the Risks Involved When Investing in Whisky?

A rule of thumb with any investment: only use money that you can spare. If the value of a whisky drops, at least you have the solace of drinking it. That is something to keep in mind when considering investing in whisky! Overproduction in the 1980s brought about a "whisky loch." A lot of fine whiskies were simply sold at low prices to rid the distilleries of overstock. Since the early 1990s things have changed and whisky's value has been rising continually. This drink is still an interesting area for investment, especially when the interest rates of savings accounts at major banks are very low.

266. What Is the Whisky Index?

The World Whisky Index was created by Dutchman Michel Kappen, a former investment banker at Rabobank with a passion for whisky. It's an index, like the Dow Jones or S&P, with the head office located at Scotch Whisky International (SWI). Its evaluation methods and criteria are not public information.

267. What Is SWI?

SWI, short for Scotch Whisky International, is a company that invests in whisky casks and bottled whisky for individual investors. Its head-quarters are based in Sassenheim, Netherlands, a mere fifteen-minute ride from Amsterdam Airport Schiphol. The company was founded by Michel Kappen and currently manages an invested fund of over €15 million (about $17 million) in whisky for a variety of clients. In 2014, SWI acquired the Zagatti collection—a unique collection of more than 3,000 bottles of whisky, carefully assembled by a famous Italian whisky aficionado. The collection is revered by many whisky enthusiasts worldwide and will be on display for visitors in 2017.

268. How Much Scotch Whisky Is Sold Annually Worldwide?

According to the Scotch Whisky Association (SWA) and International Wine and Spirits Research (IWSR), 94.1 million 9-liter cases of Scotch whisky were sold in 2015. By value rather than by volume, the United States remains the largest export market for Scotch. The sales figure includes blended and single malt for both domestic and export markets.

Above: SWI's headquarters in Sassenheim, Netherlands. *Opposite:* Whisky memorabilia: a silver quaich from the Craigellachie Hotel in Speyside and a Jack Daniel's Zippo lighter.

269. How Much American Whisky Is Sold Annually Worldwide?

According to the Distilled Spirits Council of the United States (DISCUS), 59.4 million 9-liter cases of American whiskey were sold in 2015. This is a 12.3-million-case increase since 2010. The sales figure includes both domestic and export markets.

270. What Kinds of Whisky-Related Things Can I Collect?

Most whisky distilleries sell glasses engraved with their logo, as do whisky festivals. Some brands take merchandising to another level, like Jack Daniel's. We're talking knickknacks like lapel pins, coasters, and lighters, all the way to motorbikes and electric guitars. Other brands, including Dalmore and The Macallan, sell logoed cuff links.

In addition to paraphernalia, people collect whisky books and packaging—tubes, tins, and boxes—as well as empty bottles and full miniatures. Dutchman Paul Verstappen assembled one of the world's largest miniature collections, approximately 4,000 strong. You can find out more about it at PaulsWhiskyMiniatureWorld.nl.

271. A History of Whisky Literature

In the past twenty-five years, more books on whisky have been written and published than in the past two centuries. The first serious publications on the subject began to appear in the late nineteenth century in the United Kingdom, whereas American literature came on the scene later—in the 1960s—due to the halted whisky industry during Prohibition. The following two entries describe some of the early works that are still widely used by contemporary whisky writers and deemed valuable resources. Some of these books are much sought after by collectors. You'll find a more comprehensive list of vintage and modern whisky literature in the Resources section (page 303).

272. Whisky Literature from the United Kingdom

Alfred Barnard

The first comprehensive work on whisky distilleries was written in 1886–87 by Alfred Barnard, at the time employed by *Harper's Weekly Gazette*. His *Whisky Distilleries of the United Kingdom* paints a picture of the whisky industry during the late Victorian Age in Great Britain. J. A. Nettleton can be considered the first author who treated the subject scientifically, in a hefty work titled *The Manufacture of Whisky and Plain Spirit*, originally published in 1913. The first book actually describing taste, titled *Notes on a Cellar-Book*, was written by George Saintsbury in 1920. In the next sixty years, only a few interesting general books on the subject were published by various authors. Then, in 1981, Scottish scholars Michael S. Moss and John R. Hume published the seminal work

The Making of Scotch Whisky: A History of the Scotch Whisky Distilling Industry, commemorating the centennial of Bruichladdich Distillery on the Isle of Islay. However, the most famous twentieth- and early twenty-first-century whisky writer was Michael Jackson (1942–2007). His *Malt Whisky Companion* was first released in 1989, followed by four updated editions in years to come. Most contemporary whisky writers pay tribute to these six scribes in their own works.

273. Whisky Literature from the United States

As a result of Prohibition (1920–33; see entry 178), the American whiskey industry had a serious rift in its history, and consequently whiskey books predating that period are virtually nonexistent. Thirty-two years after repeal, Frank Kane reconstructed the resurrection of the whiskey industry in his 1965 book, *Anatomy of the Whisky Business*.

The year 1968 witnessed *Whiskey in the Kitchen*, written by Emanuel and Madeline Greenberg. It was the first serious attempt to write comprehensively about the combination of whiskey and food. Oscar Getz, whose whiskey collection is housed in a dedicated museum in Bardstown, Kentucky, assembled and published *Whiskey: An American Pictorial History* in 1978. The book is adorned with unique images taken from Getz's personal collection. The author is considered a real guardian of America's distilling past.

The first serious tasting guide was written by Gary Regan and Mardee Haidin Regan in 1995 and is titled *The Book of Bourbon: And Other Fine American Whiskeys*. In 1999, Sam K. Cecil's historical book *The Evolution of the Bourbon Whiskey Industry in Kentucky* hit the shelves. It is one of the most important sources for tracing the founding dates, expansion dates, closures, and renamings of American distilleries through time. These authors set the stage for the contemporary whiskey writers in the United States.

274. Whisky Literature from Ireland, Canada, and Japan

Books on Irish, Canadian, and Japanese whisk(e)y are not as numerous as those on Scotch and American whisk(e)y. *Truths About Whisky* from 1834 is probably the oldest book on Irish whiskey, commissioned by Jameson, Power, and Roe, the main distilleries in Dublin at the time, from an author who remains unknown. In 1994, Jim Murray wrote *Classic Irish Whiskey*, considered the first comprehensive tasting guide for Irish whiskey. In 2002, Irish TV presenter Peter Mulryan followed suit with *The Whiskeys of Ireland*, describing the Irish whiskey scene in a historical context. In 2015, historian Fionnán O'Connor put out *A Glass Apart: Irish Single Pot Still Whiskey*, an in-depth scholarly research project into the history of the Irish whiskey type par excellence.

Canadian whisky had long been neglected in the writers' realm. *Canadian Whisky: The Product and the Industry* by William F. Rannie was published in 1976, and it wasn't until 2012 that it was followed by Davin de Kergommeaux's much-revered *Canadian Whisky: The Portable Expert*. The book became an instant classic, and turned De Kergommeaux into the go-to authority on Canadian whisky.

In 2006, the fifth edition of Michael Jackson's *Malt Whisky Companion* was translated into Japanese by Hideo Yamaoka, becoming the first serious piece of whisky literature available in Japanese. Soon after, in 2008, Ulf Buxrud, a Swedish whisky collector with a fondness for Japanese whisky, wrote *Japanese Whisky: Facts, Figures and Taste*. This book is considered to be the first attempt to publish a comprehensive book on whisky distilleries and distilling practices in the Land of the Rising Sun. A more recent book on Japanese whisky, is *Whisky Japan: The Essential Guide to the World's Most Exotic Whisky* by Dominic Roskrow.

275. *Malt Whisky Yearbook*

Perhaps the most important contemporary whisky publication, *Malt Whisky Yearbook*, was first put together in 2005 by Swedish writer Ingvar Ronde. He has since become the editor of each consecutive annual edition that includes features by various whisky writers and is a fixture on the whisky calendar. It is the ultimate reference guide for figures and timelines of malt whisky distilleries, and is a comprehensive at-a-glance summary of the past year in the world of whisky.

CHAPTER 7

WHISKY TRENDS

276. **The Current Whisky Landscape**

Whisky has been around for centuries and has undergone many changes over time. At first the drink was enjoyed straight from the still, immature, mixed with herbs and honey to soften the intensity. Then, slowly, more and more attention was paid to cask maturation.

In the second half of the nineteenth century, blended whisky came to the forefront. It was all the rage at the British court to blend wine with whisky—one of the biggest proponents of the trend being Queen Victoria, who regularly spiked her claret with whisky. The year 1988 witnessed an introduction of the Classic Malts, six single malts from Diageo, representing six different regions. The launch of these whiskies spearheaded the unstoppable increase in market share of the single malt category worldwide. Still, blended whisky makes up 85 percent or more of the entire market, led by Johnnie Walker. After many decades of decline, bourbon is making a comeback to the top shelf. Japan is a small but serious niche producer, and Irish whiskey has risen from the ashes like a phoenix, appropriately illustrated on the logos of Teeling and Tullamore. Craft distilling is picking up wherever there is a supply of grain, clear water, and yeast.

277. The Whiskey Scene in the United States

Americans are quite a dedicated bunch when it comes to their love for whiskey. One of the first whiskey magazines and one of the first whiskey festivals in the world were both established in the United States. The quarterly *Malt Advocate* was founded in 1992; it was renamed *Whisky Advocate* in 2011 and is still going strong, with contributions from writers around the world. WhiskyFest, started by John Hansell and Amy Westlake Hansell, has been running since 1998.

The growth of micro- or craft distilleries over the last decade is overwhelming. Due to changes in state legislation, it has become easier to acquire a distilling license. The American Distilling Institute (ADI) was founded in 2003 to promote and support craft distilling. It defines craft distillers as those who use a pot still, with or without rectification columns, for the production of spirits. The ADI recently created a Craft Certified Spirits program to assure that a craft spirit meets certain guidelines. These include being a product of an independently owned distillery where the product is physically distilled and bottled on-site and with maximum annual sales of 100,000 proof gallons (a proof gallon is 1 liquid gallon of spirits that is 50 percent alcohol at 60° Fahrenheit).

A relative newcomer organization is the American Craft Spirits Association (ACSA), founded in 2012. Voting members must be independent, licensed distillers and annually produce fewer than 750,000 proof gallons. The definition of "craft" certainly leaves room for interpretation.

Roughly estimating, nearly eight hundred craft distilleries are now spread across almost all the states, and not all of them are distilling spirit for whiskey. Most of them are in a fledgling condition and run into the challenge of needing to mature their white dog (see entry 156) for some years before it can be launched as whiskey. This drains their cash flow, and they partly manage the problem by also distilling drinks that can be bottled and consumed straight off the still, like vodka, gin, and unaged rum. A creative trend some cash-strapped distilleries inadvertently started was selling a bottle of white dog along with a 2-liter barrel for the customer to age his own whiskey in. This was so popular that even larger distilleries like Heaven Hill sell similar kits in their visitor centers now.

Other so-called distillers buy ready-made whiskey from one of the large commercial plants and label it as their own whiskey. The whiskey itself might be of good quality, but the consumer may be easily misled when reading the label. Legislation is under way to more clearly define what must be mentioned on the label and what is not allowed. The ADI has tried to combat this misleading practice with their spirit certification program. There have been 1,026 U.S. and Canadian spirits certified to date from 241 distilleries; 356 of these certified spirits are whiskey.

Another issue that hampers most of these small companies' development is the economics of scale, or lack thereof. An initial, basic setup of distillery equipment allows for smaller production, which has to do with licenses. With annual sales somewhere between 50,000 and 100,000 proof gallons, a distiller may be classified as a craft distiller in most states. As a result, output is limited and consumed mostly in the local market, since most wholesalers and distributors are not interested in carrying brands that do not have the potential (yet) to sell huge quantities. Larger "craft" distillers have gotten around this limitation by being located in states that allow larger annual volumes.

When Prohibition was repealed, one of the measures used to boost the economy and ensure whiskey quality was a rule that bourbon could be aged only in new oak barrels. Due to the growth in distilling worldwide, the demand for new and used bourbon barrels outstrips the current supply. On the one hand, this causes craft distilleries problems with getting their hands on good new barrels, and on the other, worldwide distillers are now facing a problem with used barrel supply. The U.S. government is looking at potential changes in legislation that would allow bourbon to mature in used barrels. This is not favored by all parties involved and remained hotly debated at the time of writing.

Many craft distillers switched from the 200-liter (53-gallon) barrels to smaller ones in order to speed up maturation. Smaller casks give off flavors, color, and aromas quicker than larger ones because of an increased surface-to-volume ratio. In craft distillery warehouses, 15-to 30-liter casks are common. Some experiment with the inside of the casks. Tuthilltown Distillery in Gardiner, New York, created a honeycomb structure within its barrels in order to extract even more flavors from the wood. They also blast loud music with pronounced bass lines through speakers in their warehouses. The sound waves stir the molecules inside the barrels, which supposedly accelerates maturation.

Corsair Distillery, founded by Darek and Amy Lee Bell, has taken American whiskey innovation to new limits, experimenting with all kinds of flavoring agents, mainly herbs and hops; smoking grains over hickory, white oak, and mesquite; and distilling not only traditional whiskey grains but also quinoa, buckwheat, and amaranth. They are not the only company experimenting with grains to create different styles of whiskey. For instance, High Wire Distillers in Charleston, South Carolina, has been distilling whiskey from sorghum for years.

These developments in wood, grain, and flavor illustrate that there is a movement to redefine whiskey that currently clashes with the establishment, which maintains that whiskey can be made only following strict rules (see entry 166 about straight bourbon). The former calls for changes to legislation; the latter lobbies to keep things as they have been since the repeal of Prohibition. The big players in the American whiskey industry have DISCUS (see the list of organizations in the Resources section, page 303) looking out for their interests. Since 2010, the craft distillers can belong to DISCUS as a Small Distiller Affiliate, the ADI, or the ACSA.

In the hotel and bar scene, single malts are being used in cocktails more frequently, along with bourbon and rye. Bars also offer their customers barrel-aged cocktails from 5- to 10-liter casks that held premixed (whiskey) cocktails for weeks or even months before being poured into the glass. This movement is a direct result of the distilleries that sold whiskey-aging kits to their customers.

One more trend to mention is the so-called bourbon shortage (see entry 7). An illustrative case is that of Pappy Van Winkle bourbon. The Stitzel-Weller Distillery, opened by Julian "Pappy" Van Winkle in 1935, was closed in 1972. Julian Van Winkle Jr. then resurrected a pre-Prohibition brand to which he still held the rights, Old Rip Van Winkle. At first he used stock from the old distillery to supply his brand. When that ran low about a decade later, his son, Julian III, had Buffalo Trace produce a wheated bourbon to his specifications. Because it is produced in limited quantities, it also has a restricted distribution. Real and perceived shortages have driven prices of these bottles to mythical proportions.

Some of these developments may be a passing fad; others may enter the mainstream.

Above: Striped Pig Distillery in Charleston, South Carolina, offers a bottle of white dog and a small whiskey barrel for sale. You can try to make your own barrel-aged cocktail at home. *Opposite:* Ginger beer and Famous Grouse are paired in a ready-to-drink cocktail.

278. The Whisky Scene in Scotland

Between 1824 and 1834, about 260 Scottish distillers received licenses and thus became legal producers of whisky. Twenty of these distilleries are still operational today. In the last decade of the nineteenth century, a staggering forty new distilleries were built, of which nineteen still produce whisky. Between 1955 and 1975, an additional twenty-four appeared on the scene, fourteen of which are still in business today.

Refurbished, expanded, and newly built distilleries seem to be on the upswing again. Since 2004, more than thirty new ones joined the ranks, and there seems to be no end in sight. These new kids on the block are spread all over Scotland, even outside the traditional whisky regions. The Kingdom of Fife, now home to five distilleries and several independent bottlers, is currently campaigning to be recognized as a distinct whisky region.

Although whisky without an age statement isn't really a novelty, the upsurge of single malts renewed the emphasis on age statements in the last few decades. The trend is currently shifting again, and more and more No Age Statement (NAS) whiskies are hitting the market. This is due partly to the limited availability of older whiskies, partly to growth in sales, and partly to the whisky-makers' desire to break free from the constraints of age regulations.

On par with whisky trends around the world, Scotland has witnessed the rebirth of the whisky cocktail. Moreover, rum and vodka have lost ground in favor of whisky as the most important alcoholic component of mixed drinks. Diageo, the largest exporter on the worldwide whisky market, organizes the most important world championship for mixologists. Whisky with ginger beer is the drink of the moment.

As far as whisky publications go, Scotland has been and still is the main hub. In 1998, the first British whisky journal in the world, *Whisky Magazine*, appeared on the scene. It is still published today, and it has reinvented itself over the years. New publications and resources include *Whiskeria*, *Whisky Quarterly*, and ScotchWhisky.com.

279. The Whiskey Scene in Ireland

Irish whiskey is a worldwide trend in itself, as the whiskey culture blossoms domestically. New distilleries are opening up all over the Republic, as well as in Northern Ireland. Dublin, which lacked a serious whiskey institution for more than fifty years, now proudly showcases Teeling Distillery, with a whiskey museum and an award-winning visitor center (a recognition received at the 2016 World Whiskies Awards). A projection for the coming years shows at least twenty-six more distilleries opening.

Looking at the latest decade, the sale of Irish whiskey has grown a whopping 220 percent. The Irish Whiskey Association published documents in the spring of 2015 disclosing great ambition: a 300-percent worldwide growth in Irish whiskey sales by 2030; a doubling of the export figures in the next fifteen years; a growth of whiskey tourism in Ireland from 600,000 to 800,000 visitors a year; a significant growth in whiskey industry jobs, from 500 to 6,500 employees in the coming decade; and an expected investment of more than €1 billion (about $1.1 billion) in the Irish whiskey industry during that same period. Irish whiskey has regained popularity to such an extent that Beam Global acquired the Cooley Distillery a few years ago. This didn't go unnoticed by Japanese drink giant Suntory, who purchased Beam Global in 2014 and seems to have great plans for both Irish whiskey and bourbon alike.

280. The Whisky Scene in the Netherlands

The increasing number of microdistilleries in a tiny country like the Netherlands (roughly the size of South Carolina), with a population of 17 million, is remarkable. There is one in nearly every province, whereas fifteen years ago, only two whisky distilleries existed: Zuidam, with the award-winning Millstone brand, and Frysk Hynder, in the province of Friesland/Fryslân. Both have significantly outgrown the "micro" label since. The Netherlands is also seeing an increased number of whisky festivals, big and small, throughout the year in every corner of the country—there are currently at least a dozen. And then there is the sudden popularity of the whisky cocktail. Bartenders don't only rely on old and trusted favorites like the Manhattan, Whiskey Sour, Rusty Nail, and Old-Fashioned, they also try their hand at creating innovations with distinctive single malts. Last but not least, there is an explosion of whisky in the media. Aside from four printed whisky magazines published by four different companies (one of them as old as twenty-five years), there has been an increase in blogs and online magazines, both professional and amateur, specializing in whisky. Although Jenever, a Dutch gin, is considered the native distilled spirit of the Netherlands, the country is a mature whisky market by industry standards and often receives new releases of whisky before other countries to serve as a testing ground for the rest of the world.

Following pages: Teeling Distillery in Dublin.

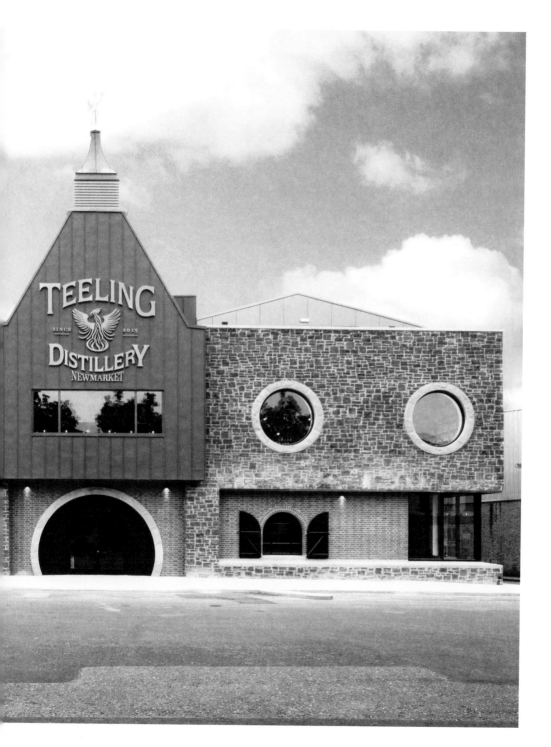

281. The Whisky Scene in Other Parts of Europe

In many European countries there is an increase in the number of small craft distilleries producing their own style of whisky. Schnapps and Obstler, spirit producers from the German-speaking countries, now distill whisky in their brandy stills, though not all whiskies from such a still are as enjoyable as their single malt Scotch whisky counterparts. The same applies to France—although high-quality whiskies from distilleries such as Warenghem and Glann Ar Mor appear on liquor store shelves throughout Europe. The Swedes put out some big-name whiskies like Mackmyra, Hven, Box, and Smögen. Founded in 1999, Mackmyra is the oldest, and visitors are welcomed to their new distillery. Their southern neighbors in Denmark attract attention with Braunstein, Fary Lochan, and Stauning, which received a £10 million (about $13 million) capital injection from Diageo. Italy recently joined the party, with the futuristic-looking Puni Distillery (see page 37).

Above: Mackmyra Distillery in Sweden. *Opposite, above:* The small Swedish island of Hven is home to Spirit of Hven Distillery, which makes not only whisky but also aquavit, vodka, and gin—and all the products are organic. *Opposite, below:* Braunstein distillery and brewery in Køge, Denmark.

282. The Whisky Scene in Japan

In Japan, whisky is often enjoyed at intimate pubs and tiny bars. There are hundreds of them, the majority so exclusive that they can host only up to twenty customers at a time. A local custom is to drink whisky out of a tall glass with lots of water and ice and to finish it in one go—a style of drinking called *mizuwari*, which literally means "mixed with water." This practice started with the drinking of *shōchū*, an indigenous distillate made from fermented rice. Japanese blended whisky (Japanese malt or grain whisky, blended with Scotch) in the twentieth century was a relatively inexpensive product. However, since the Japanese began exporting their own pure whisky, prices have gotten high. The current demand for Japanese whisky is far greater than the available stock. With around 91 million liters produced annually by only 10 distilleries, and merely 2 to 3 percent destined for export, the product is currently so scarce outside Japan that it further drives up prices. At the time of writing, there are no known plans for building new distilleries or increasing the production capacity at existing ones. But the Japanese are known for biding their time.

For years, it was rather difficult to visit Japanese distilleries, but today various companies have opened their doors to whisky tourists. In seven or eight days, it is possible to visit Chichibu, Karuizawa, Hakushu, Gotemba, and Suntory, but be prepared to arrange your own travel schedule. A nice description of such a journey is given in *World Whiskey* by Charles MacLean.

One interesting phenomenon worth noting is the Japanese purchase of American, Irish, and Scottish distilleries. Four Roses, Jim Beam, Maker's Mark, Cooley, Kilbeggan, Auchentoshan, Bowmore, Ben Nevis, Glen Garioch, and Laphroaig are all under Japanese ownership. Who knows which distillery might be next on the purchase list.

283. The Whisky Scene in Canada

Various Canadian distillers recently raised the amount of rye in their mash bills, even launching 100 percent rye whiskies onto the market. The ABV percentages have been raised as well, to between 45 to 50 percent as opposed to only 40 percent. Single barrel bottlings are beginning to see the light of day, and the growing number of microdistilleries is especially noteworthy in British Columbia, because of a change in the law there. More and more non-blended Canadian whiskies are appearing on the market too.

284. The Whisky Scene in Australasia

For many years a native distillate was consumed in many Australasian countries that did not meet all the necessary criteria to be considered "whisky." Today, these countries import mostly Scotch, next to relative newcomers in the single malt whisky segment like Amrut from India and Kavalan from Taiwan. Forsyth's, an esteemed Scottish company with a long tradition and a virtual monopoly in the industry, designed and built the Kavalan Distillery. Australia is marked by a revival of whisky distilleries, with Tasmania as the focal point. New Zealand recently built the Cardrona Distillery and museum in Wanaka—their first batch of whisky is expected in 2018 or 2019.

285. **Innovation in the Industry**

Innovation in the whisky world is often slowed down by stringent legal regulations and restrictions, especially in Scotland and the United States. New ideas are scrutinized by organizations out to preserve the established whisky traditions, most notable being the Scotch Whisky Association (SWA) and the Distilled Spirits Council of the United States (DISCUS). For example, when a Canadian distiller from Nova Scotia launched a single malt called Glen Breton, the SWA tried—in vain—to impose restrictions on the rights to the word *glen*, hoping to reserve exclusive usage for Scotch whisky.

This is not to say that innovation doesn't happen at all—on the contrary. The resulting product may not fall into the official whisky category, but the market is surely enriched by interesting beverages. Following are a few examples of new approaches in the areas of flavor, grain, and maturation.

Darek Bell is one example of a whisky industry revolutionary and rule-breaker. His craft distillery Corsair in Tennessee is a place of experimentation, where dogmatic beliefs about what kinds of grains and methods should be used in distilling are challenged. Some of his experiments with smoky flavor profiles are documented in his 2013 book *Fire Water*.

Rick Wasmund of Copper Fox Distillery in Virginia has been flavoring the grains for his whiskey with apple- and cherrywood smoke. He also puts used apple-wood and oak chips inside used bourbon barrels to influence maturation.

One of the truly great American innovators of whiskey is independent bottler and blender John Glaser, who has been on a collision course with the Scotch Whisky Association for ages. However, his experiments deal with Scotch and not with American whiskeys (to date).

But it is not only craft distillers or the occasional independent bottler who likes to experiment. Big distillers like to try new approaches, too. For instance, Buffalo Trace Distillery in Frankfort, Kentucky, has been conducting a very interesting experiment that culminated in the Single Oak Project, in which ninety-six oak trees were individually selected according to the number of growth rings per inch and the specific locations where they were harvested. Every single tree was cut into two different parts (top and bottom), resulting in 192 unique sections, from which 192 individual barrels could be made. Each barrel was charred differently prior to filling. They were then filled with different recipe whiskeys at different entry proofs and aged in different styles of warehouses. It took four years to complete the series, at which point whiskey lovers were able to compare the impact of seven different critical variables across 192 bottles with a total of 1,396 taste combinations. No bottle is the same as another in the series. After having assessed 5,086 reviews from tasters, the distillery singled out barrel #80 as the winner. This project is considered the most extensive—and probably most expensive—bourbon experiment ever conducted.

Jim Beam, another big distiller, came up with the Devil's Cut a few years ago, rinsing barrels emptied of whiskey in a patented shaking machine to get the last little bit of bourbon out and using the resulting water for diluting the bourbon. They more recently launched Double Oak, a bourbon that had a second maturation in new American oak barrels.

Even Jack Daniel's has experimented beyond flavored whiskeys. In 2014, it launched No. 27 Gold, a whiskey that matured first in charred American white oak barrels for several years, and then in maple barrels for six months to a year. Because maple barrels are much less sound than oak barrels, they tend to result in about a 20 percent angels' share—hence the short amount of time the whiskey spends in maple.

Terressentia, a relative outsider, based in Charleston, South Carolina, takes an entirely different approach that moves away from barrel aging. Instead, young whiskey is continually bombarded with ultrasonic waves and oxygen for three days. The founders claim, supported by some science, that they can reduce a twelve-year maturation time to about a week. However, most distillers aren't convinced. Maturation doesn't happen overnight; there is far more at play than moving molecules around.

286. Flavor Innovations in Whisky

Whatever some may think of them, flavored whiskies are growing in popularity. American whiskey producers started the trend when looking for ways to compete with flavored vodka for market share. Soon, various whiskey-based products started appearing one after the other. Most popular infused whiskeys taste like honey (Tennessee Honey and Jim Beam Honey), cherries (Red Stag), ginger (Virgil Kaine), cinnamon (Fireball), or Sweet Tea Bourbon (Firefly). The Scots and the Irish followed, somewhat more hesitantly, with Dewar's Highlander Honey and Bushmills Irish Honey, basically returning to a centuries-old practice.

287. What Is Craft Distilling?

Craft distilling, or *microdistilling*, is the term used for distilling on a small scale, done by innovative distilleries wanting to set themselves apart from traditional methods of production. Although their annual output is dwarfed by that of big distilling companies, their products have certainly enriched the whisky landscape as a whole in the past ten to fifteen years.

288. **The Future of Whisky**

Never before has whisky been in the public eye to the extent that it is now. Whisky clubs and organizations are gaining popularity in many countries, and festivals are too plentiful to count. The whisky industry, by nature, operates a few years in the future because the distillate matures for years before it can be sold as whisky. And who knows how much whisky will be sold in three years, let alone five or ten. There are many factors that could influence the development of the whisky world. The Far East could turn into a *mature market*, which is a term used by large manufacturers for markets that have passed both the emerging and growth phases, and where earnings and sales slow down in comparison, such as the Netherlands, Belgium, and Sweden. We have yet to see how the plethora of microdistilleries will develop. Some will survive and create a name for themselves while others will disappear because of a lack of funding or by becoming subsidiaries of large conglomerates, which is what happened to Hudson Whiskey, made by Tuthilltown Spirits Distillery in Gardiner, New York. In 2014, William Grant & Sons, of Glenfiddich and Balvenie fame, displayed an interest in bourbon and bought the brand but not the distillery. Tuthilltown is still in the hands of the founders, but its full capacity is needed for Grant's newly acquired bourbon. If the demand for whisky remains the same or increases, more small and promising distilleries are likely to follow a similar path in years to come.

Whiskey bars are popping up all over the United States, often styled as speakeasies. The Jack Rose Dining Saloon in Washington, D.C., has one in the back. In Amsterdam, guests may enter Door 74 only after having been inspected through a hatch. The growth of the number of distilleries, the increased knowledge of bartenders and sommeliers, the explosion of whisky publications, and recent takeovers show that whisky consumption will probably continue to increase in places and countries where you would not immediately expect it. A respected Scottish distilling family buys a boutique bourbon brand, the Japanese purchase Beam Global, the Mexican tequila company Cuervo acquires Northern Ireland's Bushmills from Diageo. What's next?

Opposite: At Tuthilltown, whiskey matures to the sound of loud bass music. The vibrations are supposed to positively influence maturation.

CHAPTER 8

WHISKY TRIVIA

289. **Who Invented Distilling?**

The origins of distilling are shrouded in the mists of time. In the course of history, various stories have been noted by historians, journalists, authors, and amateurs alike.

One myth favored by many states is that distilling came from ancient China, traveling via India to the Middle East—known as the Old Silk Route, which Marco Polo and his ilk took to China. Although there is no solid evidence to support this theory, there are some clues that hint to its possible validity. For example, some rudimentary distilling equipment was discovered in Iraq (formerly Mesopotamia) in the 1980s. Scientists dated their findings to around 3500 BC. The apparatus was probably used to extract scents for use in balms and essences.

Four thousand years later, the first written accounts of distilling practices appeared in the works of Islamic scholars. One among them, Geber (short for Abū Mūsā Jābir ibn Hayyān), is considered to be the father of Arabic chemistry. He made real strides in changing alchemy from magic into science and is credited with various inventions that form the basic equipment still used in modern laboratories. One of them is the alembic, a primitive distilling apparatus that is believed to be the predecessor of a modern-day pot still.

290. **Which Nation Was the First to Make Whisky?**

It is generally assumed that the Irish were the first to try their hand at making whisky. Some evidence can be found in the *Red Book of Ossory* from the early fourteenth century, attributed to the Irish bishop Richard Ledred. His is the first written Irish account of the distillation process, and on those grounds he may be dubbed the "godfather" of whisky.

Opposite: The smallest working pot still in the Scottish whisky industry can be found at Loch Ewe Distillery, on the west coast in the village of Aultbea.

291. Why Was Whisky Predominantly Distilled in Colder Regions at First?

Due to perfect climate conditions, southern Europe has been growing grapes and turning them into wine for centuries, so it makes sense that cognac, Armagnac, and brandy originate from that area. However, northern Europe's climate was much too harsh for grapes, and the main crop was barley, which is why the northern regions have a rich beer-brewing history. Putting it very simply, whisky could be thought of as nothing more than distilled beer without the hops. So the colder climates of the north had better conditions for whisky than did the warmer south.

Nowadays, whisky is made in hot climates as well, more often than not from barley or corn grown elsewhere, while vineyards can now be found as far north as the Netherlands and England.

292. How Did Whisky-Making Knowledge End Up in Ireland?

The Moors, a North African group that invaded Spain in the eighth century, spread the art of distilling through monasteries all over Europe in the wake of Christianity. This was a slow and gradual process. At the turn of the thirteenth century, the French noble family Bethune moved to Ireland and Scotland. Various members of the family were prominent physicians who had access to a huge library of medical books translated from original Arabic and Greek manuscripts into Gaelic. Distilling was a medical profession at the time, and that may be an explanation for how they came to be the disseminators of distilling knowledge.

293. **Who Was Saint Patrick?**

The Irish saint Patrick (circa 387–461) is often associated with the arrival of distilling in Ireland. His life was quite a rags-to-riches story—he went from being a slave to being a bishop. During his missionary travels, he supposedly spread his knowledge of distilling alongside the Gospel. However, this may be as much of a myth as the story of Saint Patrick banishing snakes from Ireland. (Archaeological and historical findings show there were never any snakes in Ireland to begin with.)

294. **Who Was Saint Columba?**

Another saint regularly but incorrectly associated with the origins of distilling in Ireland is Saint Columba, who followed in Saint Patrick's missionary footsteps a mere century later. He founded a Christian community on the Isle of Iona, off of Scotland's western coast, in the year 563. During his life he made many journeys between Scotland and Ireland and allegedly brought the art of distilling to the Scots. However, this theory also remains unproven.

Following pages: Iona Abbey, viewed here from the Isle of Mull, was founded by Saint Columba.

295. What Is the Oldest Distillery in Ireland?

The oldest working distillery in Ireland is Kilbeggan, located in the eponymous village in central Ireland. Built in 1757, the distillery, historically also known under the names Brusna and Locke's, had slowly been deteriorating until 1982, when a group of local enthusiasts began an intense restoration program. In 2011, after 150 years of inactivity, whisky production started up again. Kilbeggan distillery is currently owned by the Japanese company Beam Suntory.

The oldest known distilling license was issued in 1608 in County Antrim, where Bushmills Distillery was founded in 1784—however, that is in Northern Ireland.

296. How Did the Scots Learn to Distill Whisky?

It isn't known precisely when the Scots started making whisky. The art of distilling probably came from neighboring Ireland, but when exactly remains a mystery. The first written references to the process in Scotland appeared in 1494, a century later than the *Red Book of Ossory* (see entry 290). Hence the Irish claim to be the inventors of whisky; whereas the Scots pride themselves with inventing the *marketing* of whisky.

Opposite: A look inside Kilbeggan, the oldest working distillery in Ireland—and probably the world.

297. Who Was John Cor?

John Cor was a monk based in Lindores Abbey in Fife during the reign of James IV, a Scottish king who ordered him to make whisky. His name can be found in the first written reference to Scotch whisky in the 1494 register of the Exchequer: "to Friar John Cor, by order of the King, to make aqua vitae VIII bols of malt." In accepting the order, John Cor officially became the first whisky distiller in Scotland.

298. What Is the Oldest Distillery in Scotland?

In Scotland, there is still a handful of working distilleries dating back to the eighteenth century: Balblair, Glen Garioch, Tobermory, Bowmore, Strathisla, and Glenturret. The oldest one is thought to be Glenturret, founded in 1775.

299. How Did Whiskey Distilling Come to the United States?

When the first settlers crossed the Atlantic from England, they took rye and barley seeds with them to grow crops for baking bread and brewing beer. Since distilling was already a common practice in Europe at the time, they probably brought the odd copper pot still with them too. Pioneers soon discovered that barley didn't grow well in New England but rye did. As a consequence, the first American whiskey was distilled mainly from rye in Pennsylvania's Monongahela Valley (which is why rye whiskey is sometimes called Monongahela whiskey). However, corn slowly became the dominant grain for whiskey-making, when Native Americans introduced the settlers to indigenous corn.

300. What Was the Whiskey Rebellion?

In the eighteenth century, distilling whiskey was a way for American farmers to use up their grain surplus. Whiskey rapidly became a commodity and was used as a currency in bartering for clothing, food, and other daily necessities. Whiskey also had a much higher value than unprocessed grain, not to mention the fact that a barrel of whiskey was far easier to transport than bushels of grain.

When the country gained its independence from England after the American Revolutionary War (1775–83), the brand-new Union was confronted with an enormous economic deficit caused by the eight-year conflict. The federal government decided to introduce a whiskey tax in the hopes of repaying some of its war debts (a somewhat ironic plan considering the war began over a tax issue with the English).

For numerous small-farm distilleries in Pennsylvania and Virginia, this posed a real problem. They used whiskey as their currency, didn't receive cash for it, could not pay the imposed tax, and chose to ignore it altogether, which got them in trouble with the government. Federal officials were deployed to force the farmers to go to court. Many of them would have to travel hundreds of miles to do so. They refused point blank. Besides the fact that they had no intention whatsoever of paying these fines, the journey was also a perilous one. Before they would reach the relative safety of Philadelphia, their trip would lead them through various areas where hostile Native Americans lived. Instead, the farmers rebelled, chased away the government officials, burned their houses, and even threatened to kill their families. Clearly, the government could not allow such behavior, and 15,000 troops were sent to the region to restore law and order. The Whiskey Rebellion, also referred to as the Whiskey Insurrection, was soon snuffed out like a candle in the wind.

301. What Did the First President of the United States Have to Do with Whiskey?

Besides being largely responsible for nipping the Whiskey Rebellion in the bud, in the last years of his life, George Washington was a rather successful whiskey distiller, albeit with a Scottish distillery manager at his side. At his Mount Vernon estate, he distilled a considerable amount of whiskey and made substantial profits from it. After his demise, however, the distillery soon fell into ruins. It was only in the twenty-first century that the historic complex was restored, and it is now a featured tourist attraction. Occasionally, small amounts of whiskey are distilled at Mount Vernon.

Above: A reenactor in the fully restored Mount Vernon Distillery.
Opposite: General Washington and his troops near Fort Cumberland, Maryland, before their march to suppress the Whiskey Rebellion in western Pennsylvania.

302. **What Is Moonshining?**

Distilling whiskey illegally is called moonshining. The practice used to take place in hiding, by the light of the moon, throughout the wooded hills of Tennessee, the Carolinas, and Georgia, as well as in the lowlands near the coast.

Moonshine is colorless, but it should not be confused with white dog, as the legal fresh distillate is called in the United States. Moonshining still takes place today in urban as well as remote environments.

303. **What Does NASCAR Have to Do with Moonshine?**

To escape the police when pursued, moonshiners customized the engines of their cars to give them more power, unknowingly creating the foundation for car races later held in the NASCAR circuit.

304. **Who Was Elijah Craig?**

Reverend and businessman Elijah Craig (1738–1808) is often credited as the inventor of bourbon. He was allegedly the first person to char the inside of the barrels, and by doing so he improved the taste of bourbon. However, documents exist showing that whiskey was made and matured in Virginia and Kentucky before Craig's time.

305. **Who Was Evan Williams?**

This American from Virginia built the first commercial distillery in the country, in 1783, in an area that in 1792 would become the Commonwealth of Kentucky. His name lives on in Evan Williams Kentucky Straight Bourbon Whiskey.

306. **Who Was Jack Daniel?**

Jack Daniel was just a boy when he ran away from his home in Tennessee to escape his stepmother. He was hired by Dan Call, a storekeeper and lay preacher who also made whiskey in a barn at his farm. Call planned to teach young Jack all about making whiskey, reportedly saying: "You will become the best whiskey maker in the world." When Call's wife and the parish forced him to choose between spirit and the Spirit, he chose the latter and left the stills to Jack. That was around 1863, and in 1866 Jack registered his distillery. Today, Jack Daniel's is the bestselling American whiskey worldwide, with an annual production of approximately 140 million liters, about half of which is exported to Europe. Not a bad outcome for a company whose founder was a runaway.

307. **Who Was James Crow?**

In 1833, the Old Oscar Pepper Distillery in Frankfort, Kentucky, hired the Scottish-born chemist and physicist Dr. James Crow. In the subsequent twenty-two years, James Crow dedicated his career to the improvement of the distilling process and developed a series of measuring instruments that immediately earned recognition with many other distillers. Crow left his mark on process hygiene too. He experimented with various levels of barrel-charring to influence the maturation process, creating a standard still in use today. He is also credited with the introduction of the sour mash method (see entry 149).

Old Oscar Pepper is fully restored and quickly became one of the showcases of the American whiskey industry. Its current name is Woodford Reserve Distillery.

308. **Who Was John Jameson?**

John Jameson was born in Scotland in 1749. At the age of twenty-one he moved to Dublin, where he mingled with other whiskey distillers, eventually starting Bow Street Distillery in 1780. Thus, Ireland's bestselling whiskey brand was born. For more than two centuries, a descendant of the Jameson family stood at the helm of the company, until 1988, when the French company Pernod Ricard took over. The production of Jameson had already been moved away from Dublin to Midleton in County Cork. This new distillery produces a whole range of brands, among which are Paddy and the single pot still whiskeys Redbreast and Green Spot. The original Jameson distillery buildings in Dublin were abandoned and neglected until 2007, when the whole complex was restored for €5 million (about $5.6 million). The result is the Old Jameson Distillery—a beautiful museum with a fine restaurant.

309. **Who Was James Power?**

James Power founded the John's Lane Distillery in Dublin in 1791. He would become one of Jameson's fiercest competitors. The rivalry went on until 1966, when the Power and Jameson families merged their businesses into the Irish Distillers Group. Pernod Ricard acquired that group some twenty years later. Powers whiskey is a tipple of choice in Ireland but is gaining recognition outside its borders. As with Jameson, production was moved to Midleton, County Cork, in the 1970s. Remnants of this huge distillery can still be seen at the National College of Art and Design (see page 125).

310. **Who Was Robert Stein?**

Robert Stein is credited as the inventor of the column still, created in 1827. His compatriot Aeneas Coffey later took credit for improving the invention and patented it under his own name (see entry 138).

Above: Authentic Coffey stills in the courtyard of Locke's Distillery in the village of Kilbeggan, Ireland. *Opposite, above:* The twin pagoda at Ardbeg Distillery on Islay has been converted into a cozy restaurant and gift shop.

311. Who Was Charles Doig?

Charles C. Doig (1855–1918) was the most famous Scottish distillery architect of the late Victorian Age. He is known for having designed more than fifty-five distilleries. His name lives on in the Doig Ventilator, a device he created to improve the airflow in the kiln's chimney. The

roof of his ventilator is distinctly pagoda-shaped and was designed using the "golden ratio," thus pleasing to the eye. Dailuaine Distillery is said to have received the first pagoda roof, in 1889. Within a couple of years, most distilleries followed suit.

312. Who Was Robert Burns?

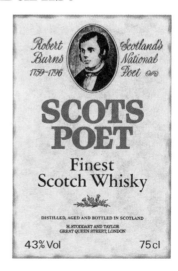

Robert "Rabbie" Burns (1759–1796) is Scotland's most famous poet. His name is inextricably linked to whisky and food. His birthday, January 25, is commemorated all over the world with a festive celebration called "Burns Supper." The highlight of the supper is the reciting of "Address to a Haggis," his ode to the traditional Scottish dish, followed by a toast to the haggis made with a fine glass of whisky. Pouring some of the golden liquid over the haggis is common practice too.

313. **Who Was Shinjiro Torii?**

The founding father of the Japanese whisky industry was born in Osaka in 1879. In 1899 he started studying the art of blending, at first with wines. This led in 1907 to his first "Western" product, a sweet fortified wine called Akadama Port Wine—a beverage that became the pillar of his company.

At that time, whisky was imported from Scotland, so in 1923 Torii invested in the creation of his own whisky distillery and named it Yamazaki. It was the forerunner of the current Suntory, a company with serious interests in the Scottish whisky industry (Auchentoshan, Bowmore, Laphroaig, and Glen Garioch) as well as the Irish (Cooley, Locke's, and Kilbeggan), which also owns Beam Global (Jim Beam, Maker's Mark, and Canadian Club). The name Suntory is derived from the Japanese flag, with its rising sun, and the last name of the original founder.

314. **Who Was Masataka Taketsuru?**

In 1918, twenty-four-year-old Masataka Taketsuru left his home country for Scotland—he would learn how the Scots made their whisky.

He returned to Japan two years later, not only with a wealth of notes and knowledge about distilling, but also with a Scottish spouse, Jessie Roberta Cowan—Rita for short. He joined Shinjiro Torii and in 1923 helped build the Yamazaki distillery, where he would work for the next decade. In 1934 he decided to build his own distillery and moved to Yoichi, on the island of Hokkaidō in northern Japan. He followed the traditional Scottish distilling methods, kept in touch with his mentors, and finally produced his own whisky, Nikka. Taketsuru passed away in 1979 at the ripe old age of eighty-five. In 1989, Nikka purchased the Ben Nevis Distillery in Fort William, Scotland.

315. Who Is Tatsuya Minagawa?

Tatsuya Minagawa is probably the most well-known contemporary ambassador of Japanese whisky. In the 1990s, he came to Scotland and applied for a job as bartender at the famous Craigellachie Hotel in the village of the same name. Some years later, he switched allegiances and went to work in the Highlander Inn, opposite the hotel. A few years ago, Suntory offered him a position as whisky ambassador for Western Europe, a title he gladly accepted and held for some time. Becoming a renowned whisky connoisseur, he was eventually offered a position as co-owner of the Highlander Inn, which brought him back to Craigellachie, the place where he began his career in the whisky industry. Tatsuya Minagawa is a sought-after guest at many whisky festivals, beloved for his master classes and deep knowledge of whisky in general, and Japanese whisky in particular.

316. Who Was Hiram Walker?

Hiram Walker (1816–99), an American businessman, was the founder of Hiram Walker and Sons Ltd., a company that would grow into one of the main companies in the Canadian whisky industry. Canadian Club, originally labeled Hiram Walker's Club Whisky, remains one of the bestselling brands

of Canadian whisky. The company is currently owned by Beam Suntory, part of the Japanese Suntory Holdings Ltd. Hiram Walker is considered one of the five founding fathers of the Canadian whisky industry, along with James Gooderham Worts, Henry Corby, Joseph Seagram, and J. P. Wiser.

317. Who Was Samuel Bronfman?

Sam Bronfman (1889–1971) emigrated with his parents from Russia to Canada at an early age. When his father purchased a hotel in 1903, young Sam soon noticed that the real money was in liquor. His first paid job in the industry was with a distributor, but in 1924 he founded his own company, the Distillers Corporation Limited. This was during Prohibition in the United States, and Bronfman is said to have earned many millions by smuggling, or at least aiding the smuggling, of Canadian whisky south of the border. The story rings all the more true when one considers the fact that Bronfman managed to acquire Canadian distiller Seagram's in 1928. He further invested in whisky worldwide, purchasing, among other brands, Chivas Regal in Scotland. Bronfman was a man of extremes, respected and feared at the same time—cold and hard as stone in business, but also a great philanthropist. After his demise, his two sons built Seagram's into a major international company. Bronfman's grandson sold the beverage division to Pernod Ricard at the turn of the twenty-first century, after which he invested his money in Vivendi, an internationally operating entertainment-industry conglomerate. That marked the end of the Bronfmans in the whisky industry. The family name lives on in the Samuel and Saidye Bronfman Family Foundation, a philanthropic organization in Canada.

Opposite: The Highlander Inn in Craigellachie, Scotland, is a favorite meeting place for international whisky tourists.

CHAPTER 9

WHISKY DISTILLERIES AND MAPS

318. **What Is Distillery Character?**

Each distillery has specific characteristics contributing to the unique flavor profile of its distillate. This is called the distillery character. The master distiller may experiment by altering fermentation times, changing the phenolic contents of the malted barley (see entry 47), or choosing particular types of casks (see entry 99), but the basic note of the whisky, defining its character, will almost always stay recognizable.

319. **Distilleries in Scotland**

Scottish single malts have been classified by region for a long time. The most common classification is the one used by the Scotch Whisky Association (see Resources, page 303): Highlands, Speyside, Lowlands, Islay, and Campbeltown. Islands is considered a separate region by some, but it is not officially recognized as such. Originally this regional division was an indication of the flavor profile of the whisky. Islay used to be known for its distinctive smoky single malts, and Speyside for malts with floral and fruity character. Nowadays, however, you can find

smoky Speyside malts as well as Islay whiskies that are made without peated malted barley. Still, the regional division is helpful informa-tion for those planning a visit to a specific distillery. The following is a list of Scottish malt distilleries.

Previous page: Aberfeldy Distillery, Perthshire. *Above:* Strathisla, the oldest working distillery in the Speyside region.

1. Aberfeldy (Highlands)
2. Aberlour (Speyside)
3. Abhainn Dearg (Islands)
4. Ailsa Bay (Lowlands)
5. Allt-a-Bhainne (Speyside)
6. Annandale (Lowlands)
7. Arbikie (Highlands)
8. Ardbeg (Islay)
9. Ardmore (Highlands)
10. Ardnahoe (Islay)
11. Ardnamurchan (Highlands)
12. Arran (Islands)
13. Auchentoshan (Lowlands)
14. Auchroisk (Speyside)
15. Aultmore (Speyside)
16. Balblair (Highlands)
17. Ballindalloch (Speyside)
18. Balmenach (Speyside)
19. Balvenie (Speyside)
20. Banff (Highlands)
21. Ben Nevis (Highlands)
22. BenRiach (Speyside)
23. Benrinnes (Speyside)
24. Benromach (Speyside)
25. Ben Wyvis (Highlands)
26. Bladnoch (Lowlands)
27. Blair Athol (Highlands)
28. Bowmore (Islay)
29. Braeval (Speyside)
30. Brora (Highlands)
31. Bruichladdich (Islay)
32. Bunnahabhain (Islay)
33. Caol Ila (Islay)
34. Caperdonich (Speyside)
35. Cardhu (Speyside)
36. Clynelish (Highlands)
37. Coleburn (Speyside)
38. Convalmore (Speyside)
39. Cragganmore (Speyside)
40. Craigellachie (Speyside)
41. Daftmill (Lowlands)
42. Dailuaine (Speyside)
43. Dallas Dhu (Speyside)
44. Dalmore (Highlands)
45. Dalmunach (Speyside)
46. Dalwhinnie (Highlands, Speyside)
47. Deanston (Highlands)
48. Dufftown (Speyside)
49. Duncan Taylor (Highlands)

50. Eden Mill (Lowlands)
51. Edradour (Highlands)
52. Falkirk (Lowlands)
53. Fettercairn (Highlands)
54. Gartbreck (Islay)
55. Glasgow (Lowlands)
56. Glen Albyn (Highlands)
57. Glenallachie (Speyside)
58. Glenburgie (Speyside)
59. Glencadam (Highlands)
60. GlenDronach (Highlands)
61. Glendullan (Speyside)
62. Glen Elgin (Speyside)
63. Glenesk (Highlands)
64. Glenfarclas (Speyside)
65. Glenfiddich (Speyside)
66. Glen Flagler (Lowlands)
67. Glen Garioch (Highlands)
68. Glenglassaugh (Highlands)
69. Glengoyne (Lowlands, Highlands)
70. Glen Grant (Speyside)
71. Glengyle (Campbeltown)
72. Glen Keith (Speyside)
73. Glenkinchie (Lowlands)
74. Glenlivet (Speyside)
75. Glenlochy (Highlands)
76. Glenlossie (Speyside)
77. Glen Mhor (Highlands)
78. Glenmorangie (Highlands)
79. Glen Moray (Speyside)
80. Glen Ord (Highlands)
81. Glenrothes (Speyside)
82. Glen Scotia (Campbeltown)
83. Glen Spey (Speyside)
84. Glentauchers (Speyside)
85. Glenturret (Highlands)
86. Glenugie (Highlands)
87. Glenury Royal (Highlands)
88. Highland Park (Islands)
89. Imperial (Speyside)
90. Inchdairnie (Lowlands)
91. Inchgower (Speyside)
92. Inverleven (Lowlands)
93. Isle of Barra (Islands)
94. Isle of Harris (Islands)
95. Jura (Islands)
96. Kilchoman (Islay)
97. Killyloch (Lowlands)
98. Kinclaith (Lowlands)

99. Kingsbarns (Lowlands)
100. Kininvie (Speyside)
101. Knockando (Speyside)
102. Knockdhu (Speyside)
103. Ladyburn (Lowlands)
104. Lagavulin (Islay)
105. Laphroaig (Islay)
106. Linkwood (Speyside)
107. Littlemill (Lowlands)
108. Loch Ewe (Highlands)
109. Loch Lomond (Highlands)
110. Lochside (Highlands)
111. Longmorn (Speyside)
112. Macallan (Speyside)
113. Macduff (Highlands)
114. Mannochmore (Speyside)
115. Millburn (Highlands)
116. Miltonduff (Speyside)
117. Mortlach (Speyside)
118. North Port/Brechin (Highlands)
119. Oban (Highlands)
120. (Old) Pulteney (Highlands)
121. Parkmore (Speyside)
122. Pittyvaich (Speyside)
123. Port Ellen (Islay)

124. Rosebank (Lowlands)
125. Roseisle (Highlands)
126. Royal Brackla (Highlands)
127. Royal Lochnagar (Highlands)
128. St. Magdalene, aka Linlithgow (Lowlands)
129. Scapa (Islands)
130. Speyburn (Speyside)
131. Speyside (Highlands, Speyside)
132. Springbank (Campbeltown)
133. Strathearn (Highlands)
134. Strathisla (Speyside)
135. Strathmill (Speyside)
136. Talisker (Islands)
137. Tamdhu (Speyside)
138. Tamnavulin (Speyside)
139. Teaninich (Highlands)
140. Tobermory (Islands)
141. Tomatin (Highlands)
142. Tomintoul (Speyside)
143. Torabhaig (Islands)
144. Tormore (Speyside)
145. Tullibardine (Highlands)
146. Wolfburn (Highlands)

Opposite: Dalwhinnie, the highest distillery in Scotland, produces a single malt with a signature honey note.

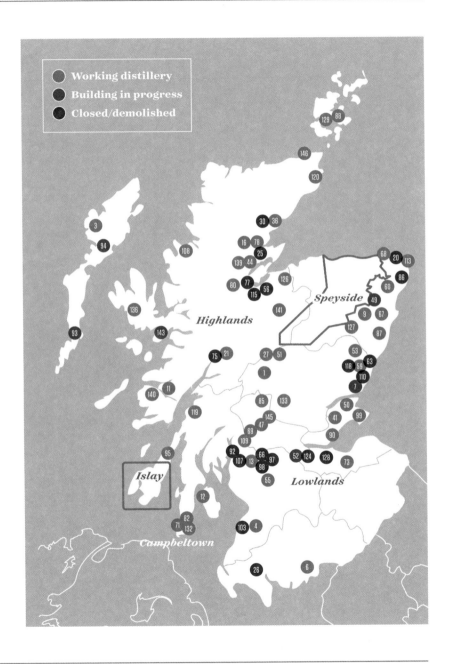

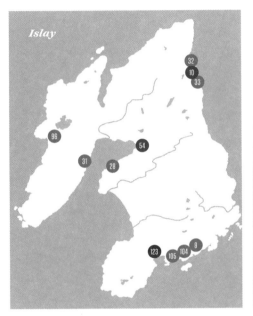

Laphroaig, Lagavulin, and Ardbeg are called the Kildalton Distilleries because of their proximity to the eighth-century Kildalton Cross. One side displays Celtic figures, the other side Christian images. This so-called high cross may be the best-preserved example of its kind and resembles similar crosses on the Isle of Iona (see entry 294) from the same period in history.

Speyside

The Spey is the fastest running river in Scotland and
lent its name to a whole whisky region.

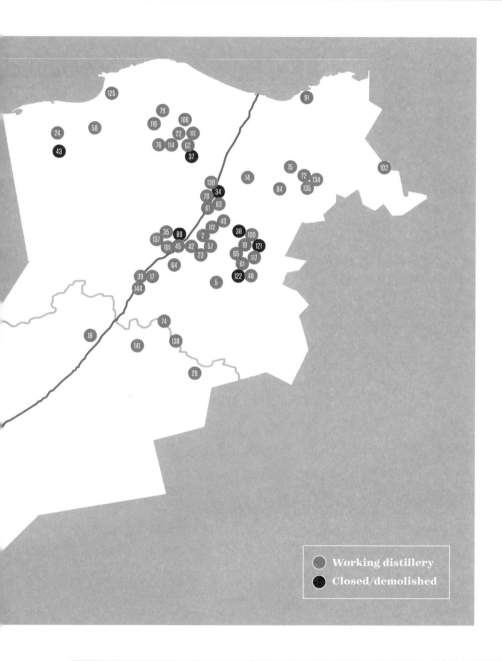

Working distillery
Closed/demolished

320. **Distilleries in Ireland**

Ireland does not use a regional classification at all. However, we have to distinguish between the Republic of Ireland and Northern Ireland. Not long ago, only three distilleries in the Republic of Ireland produced whiskey: Midleton in Cork, Cooley on the Cooley Peninsula, and Kilbeggan in Kilbeggan. Over the past five years or so, there has been a serious growth in small craft distilleries, among them Alltech/Carlow and Teeling.

For a long time, Northern Ireland had only one distillery, Bushmills in County Antrim, which is now joined by Echlinville in Belfast. The following is a list of Irish distilleries; the number is expected to grow in the next few years.

1. Alltech/Carlow
2. Belfast
3. Bushmills
4. Cooley
5. Dingle
6. Echlinville
7. Great Northern
8. Midleton
9. Kilbeggan
10. Pearse Lyons
11. Teeling Whiskey Company
12. Tullamore Dew
13. Walsh Whiskey
14. Waterford Distillery
15. West Cork Distillers

Bushmills visitor center in County Antrim, Northern Ireland.

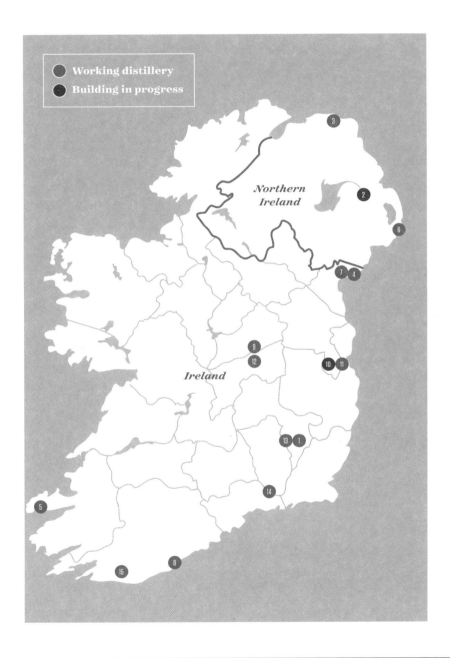

Working distillery

Building in progress

Northern Ireland

Ireland

321. **Distilleries in England and Wales**

Both England and Wales were without a single whisky distillery for more than a century. As the new era of British whisky started, in 2004 the first distillery to open its doors was Penderyn, located in proximity of the Brecon Beacons Park in South Wales. St George's Distillery in Norwich followed in 2006. The Lakes Distillery, London Distillery Company, Adnams, Hicks & Healey, and Cotswolds Distillery joined the ranks in recent years. More growth is expected in this part of the world too. Wales and England do not use a regional specification.

The following is a list of distilleries in England and Wales.

1. Adnams
2. Bimber
3. The Cotswolds Distillery
4. Dartmoor Whisky
5. Hicks & Healey

6. The Lakes Distillery
7. The London Distillery Company
8. Penderyn
9. St George's Distillery
10. Spirit of Yorkshire

One of the St George's Distillery warehouses in Norwich, East Anglia, England.

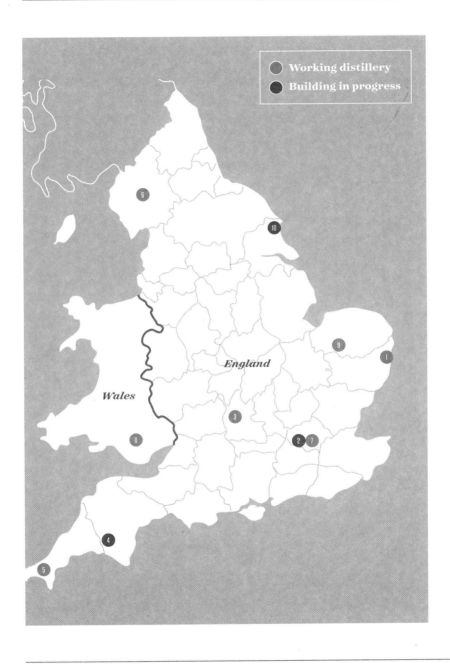

322. Distilleries in the United States

The state of Kentucky, home of the big bourbons, has the largest concentration of whiskey distilleries in the United States. It's there you'll find Barton 1792 Distillery, Buffalo Trace, Four Roses, Heaven Hill, Jim Beam, Maker's Mark, Wild Turkey, and Woodford Reserve distilleries, all in relatively close proximity to one another. This concentration was caused by Prohibition (see entry 178) in the 1920s. After the repeal in 1933, the entire industry had to be rebuilt nearly from scratch. The few big players like Schenley Corporation, the Sazerac family, and the Shapiro Brothers joined forces and rebuilt the Kentucky distillery scene, which resulted in this cluster. Only very recently was the old Stitzel-Weller Distillery of Pappy Van Winkle fame brought back to life by its current owner, Diageo.

In Tennessee you can find Jack Daniel's and George Dickel within a half-hour drive of each other. Prichard's in Kelso is not too far away either.

A nameless distillery complex in Indiana, formerly owned by Seagram's and now by MGP, produces huge amounts of whiskey and bourbon for private labels and various craft distilleries.

Spread across the entire United States you will find craft distilleries in almost every state. Their numbers run into the hundreds. This growth was mainly caused by a change in the law that made it easier to acquire a distilling license. Roughly 25 percent of 800 registered craft distilleries are producing their own whiskeys or have plans to do so, and distribution is usually limited. Kentucky and Tennessee remain the states with the highest concentration of large-production whiskey distilleries.

The website Sku's Recent Eats tries to maintain an up-to-date overview, organized by state. The following is a non-exhaustive list of well-known whiskey distilleries per state.

Opposite, above: The picturesque visitor center of Woodford Reserve in Versailles, Kentucky. *Opposite, below:* Jim Beam's Clermont distillery in Kentucky is a huge industrial complex.

KENTUCKY
1. Barton 1792 Distillery (Bardstown)
2. Brown-Forman (Louisville)
3. Buffalo Trace Distillery (Frankfort)
4. Bulleit (Louisville)
5. Four Roses (Lawrenceburg)
6. Heaven Hill (Louisville and Bardstown)
7. Jim Beam (Clermont)
8. Maker's Mark (Loretto)
9. Wathen's (Owensboro)
10. Wild Turkey (Lawrenceburg)
11. Willett Distillery (Bardstown)
12. Woodford Reserve (Versailles)

TENNESSEE
13. Corsair Distillery (Nashville)
14. George Dickel (Tullahoma)
15. Jack Daniel's (Lynchburg)
16. Prichard's Distillery (Kelso)

ALABAMA
17. Big Escambia Spirits (Atmore)
18. Irons Distillery (Huntsville)

ALASKA
19. Alaska Distillery (Wasilla)
20. Anchorage Distillery (Anchorage)

ARIZONA
21. Arizona Distilling Company (Tempe)
22. Hamilton Distillers (Tucson)

ARKANSAS
23. Arkansas Moonshine (Newport)
24. Rock Town Distillery (Little Rock)

CALIFORNIA
25. Anchor Distilling Company (San Francisco)
26. Charbay (St. Helena)

COLORADO
27. Wood's High Mountain Distillery (Salida)
28. Stranahans (Denver)

CONNECTICUT
29. Elm City Distillery (Wallingford)
30. Onyx Spirits Co. (East Hartford)

DELAWARE
31. Painted Stave Distilling (Smyrna)

FLORIDA
32. Key West Distilling (Key West)
33. St. Augustine Distillery (St. Augustine)

GEORGIA
34. Dalton Distillers (Dalton)
35. Thirteenth Colony Distilleries (Americus)

IDAHO
36. 8 Feathers Distillery (Boise)
37. Idaho Bourbon Distillers (Boise)

ILLINOIS
38. Koval Distillery (Chicago)
39. Quincy Street Distillery (Riverside)

INDIANA
40. 12.05 Distillery (Indianapolis)
41. Midwest Grain Products Ingredients (Lawrenceburg)

IOWA
42. Cedar Ridge Winery & Distillery (Swisher)
43. Templeton Rye (Templeton)

KANSAS
44. High Plains Distillery (Atchison)
45. Union Horse Distilling Co. (Lenexa)

LOUISIANA
46. Atelier Vie (New Orleans)
47. Louisiana Lightning LLC (Amite)

MAINE
48. Liquid Riot Bottling Co. (Portland)
49. Wiggly Bridge Distillery (York)

MARYLAND
50. Fiore Distillery (Pylesville)
51. Old Line Spirits (Baltimore)

MASSACHUSETTS
52. Berkshire Mountain Distillers (Great Barrington)
53. Bully Boy Distillery (Boston)

MICHIGAN
54. Journeyman (Three Oaks)
55. New Holland Brewing Co. (Holland)

MINNESOTA
56. Eleven Wells (St. Paul)
57. Millers & Saints Distillery (St. Louis Park)

MISSISSIPPI
58. Cathead Distillery (Jackson)
59. Sweet Water Distillery (Sandy Hook)

MISSOURI
60. Copper Run Distillery (Walnut Shade)
61. T's Redneck Distillery (Lebanon)

MONTANA
62. Glacier Distilling (Coram)
63. Rattlesnake Creek Distillers (Missoula)

NEBRASKA
64. Cut Spike Distillery (La Vista)

NEVADA
65. Branded Hearts Distillery (Reno)
66. Seven Troughs Distilling (Sparks)

NEW HAMPSHIRE
67. Djinn Spirits (Nashua)
68. Tamworth Distilling (Tamworth)

NEW JERSEY
69. Claremont Distillery, (Fairfield)
70. Jersey Spirits Distilling Co. (Fairfield)

NEW MEXICO
71. Don Quixote Distillery (Los Alamos)
72. Santa Fe Spirits Distillery (Santa Fe)

NEW YORK
73. Long Island Spirits (Baiting Hollow)
74. Tuthilltown Spirits (Gardiner)

NORTH CAROLINA
75. Blue Ridge Distilling Co. (Bostic)
76. Foothills Distillery (Conover)

OHIO
77. Canal Spirits Craft Distillery (Canal Fulton)
78. Watershed Distillery (Columbus)

OKLAHOMA
79. Scissortail Distillery (Moore)

OREGON
80. Clear Creek (Portland)
81. Rogue Spirits (Newport)

PENNSYLVANIA
82. County Seat Spirits (Allentown)
83. Pittsburgh Distilling Co. (Pittsburgh)

RHODE ISLAND
84. Sons of Liberty Spirits Co. (South Kingstown)

SOUTH CAROLINA
85. High Wire Distilling (Charleston)
86. Striped Pig Distillery (Charleston)

SOUTH DAKOTA
87. Dakota Spirits Distillery (Pierre)

TEXAS
88. Balcones Distilling (Waco)
89. Yellow Rose Distilling (Houston)

UTAH
90. High West Distillery (Port City)

VERMONT
91. Appalachian Gap Distillery (Middlebury)
92. WhistlePig (Shoreham)

VIRGINIA
93. A. Smith Bowman (Fredericksburg)
94. Copper Fox Distillery (Sperryville)
95. George Washington Distillery (Mount Vernon)

WASHINGTON
96. 2bar Spirits (Seattle)
97. Woodinville Whiskey Co. (Woodinville)

WASHINGTON, D.C.
98. One Eight Distilling

WEST VIRGINIA
99. Black Draft Distillery (Martinsburg)
100. West Virginia Distilling Co. (Morgantown)

WISCONSIN
101. 45th Parallel Distillery (New Richmond)
102. Death's Door Spirits (Middleton)

Working distillery

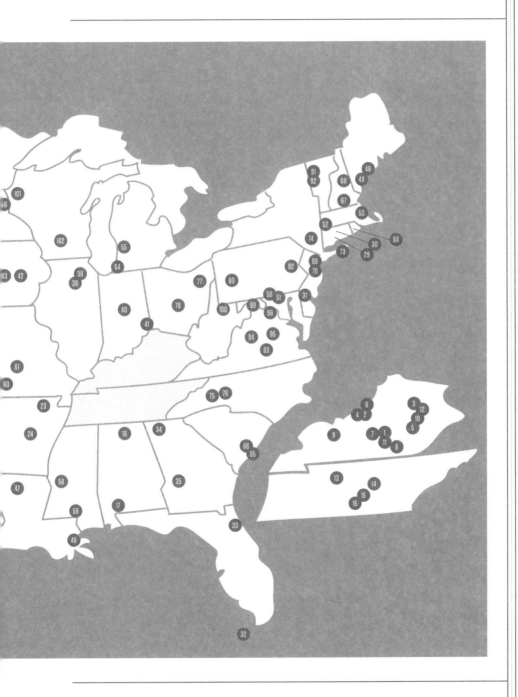

323. Distilleries in Canada

The large Canadian distilleries are not very welcoming to whisky tourists. They are spread all over the country: Highwood, Black Velvet, and Alberta Distillers in Alberta; Gimli in Manitoba; Hiram Walker, Canadian Mist, and Forty Creek in Ontario; and last but not least, Valleyfield in Quebec. Each one of these uses its own methods of production, but one cannot speak of a specific region or "terroir" that would define the character of the whisky. Glenora, distilled in Nova Scotia, was the first Canadian single malt whisky.

The following is a non-exhaustive list of all major and some craft distilleries in Canada.

1. Alberta Distillers
2. Black Velvet
3. Canadian Mist
4. Gimli
5. Glenora

6. Highwood Distillers
7. Hiram Walker & Sons
8. Forty Creek Distillery
9. Valleyfield

Prior to 1984, Highwood Distillers in the Canadian Rocky Mountains was called "Sunnyvale."

324. Distilleries in Japan

Japan has been making whisky for nearly a century now and counts eleven working distilleries, Yamazaki being the oldest. The other ten—Chichibu, Fuji-Gotemba, Hakushu, Hanyu, Karuizawa, Miyashita Shuzo, Miyagikyo, Mars Shinshu, White Oak, and Yoichi—can be found all over the country. Yoichi is the northernmost distillery, located on the island of Hokkaidō. The following is a list of Japanese distilleries.

1. Akkeshi
2. Chichibu
3. Chita
4. Fuji-Gotemba
5. Hakushu
6. Hanyu
7. Karuizawa
8. Mars Shinshu
9. Miyagikyo
10. Miyashita Shuzo
11. Shizuoka
12. White Oak
13. Yamazaki
14. Yoichi

Above: Miyagikyo Distillery in the Miyagi region of Japan was founded in 1969.
Following pages: The Craigellachie Hotel in Speyside, Scotland, with its famous Quaich Bar attracts whisky lovers from around the world.

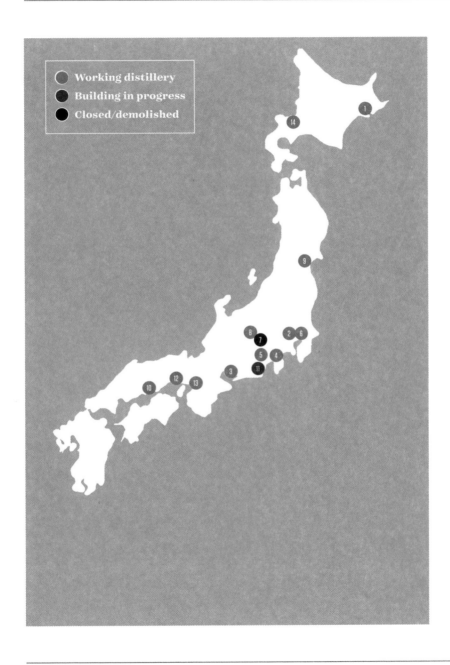

Some Drinking Recommendations

Finally, the only thing left to do is to start exploring the vast whisky world, one glass at a time. Whether you're a complete novice to whisky and don't know where to start or you want to try whiskies with different levels of smokiness, explore American whiskeys beyond Bourbon, or expand your usual go-to list with some international favorites, here are a few must-try recommendations to get you going.

A GOOD PLACE TO START
1. Glen Grant Major's Reserve
2. Glenfiddich 12-year-old
3. The Glenlivet 12-year-old
4. Aberlour 10-year-old
5. Dalwhinnie 15-year-old
6. GlenDronach 15-year-old
7. Glenrothes Select Reserve
8. Glenmorangie Lasanta
9. Dalmore 15-year-old
10. The Macallan 12-year-old Sherry Oak

LIGHTLY PEATED AND MARITIME WHISKIES
1. Oban 14-year-old
2. Old Pulteney 17-year-old
3. Clynelish 14-year-old
4. Scapa 16-year-old
5. Springbank 10-year-old

HEAVILY PEATED WHISKIES
1. Bowmore 12-year-old
2. Talisker Dark Storm
3. Lagavulin 16-year-old
4. Ardbeg Uigeadail
5. Laphroaig 10-year-old

ALL-TIME FAVORITES
1. Highland Park 18-year-old
2. Glenfarclas 15-year-old
3. The Glenlivet 21-year-old
4. Glenmorangie 18-year-old
5. The Balvenie DoubleWood

GET YOUR BOURBON STRAIGHT
1. Maker's Mark
2. Eagle Rare 10-year-old
3. Jim Beam Double Oak
4. 1792 Ridgemont Reserve
5. Elijah Craig 12-year-old

GET YOUR BOURBON STRAIGHTER
1. Four Roses Single Barrel
2. Blanton's Single Barrel
3. Knob Creek
4. Booker's
5. Wild Turkey 101

BEYOND BOURBON
1. Stranahan's Colorado Whiskey
2. Jack Daniel's Single Barrel
3. Bulleit Rye Whiskey
4. George Dickel No. 12
5. Old Overholt Rye

BLENDED SCOTCHES DELUXE
1. Chivas Regal 18-year-old
2. Johnnie Walker Green 15-year-old
3. Ballantine's 17-year-old
4. Dewar's 18-year-old
5. Compass Box Spice Tree

IRISH WHISKEYS
1. Jameson
2. Tyrconnell
3. Writers Tears
4. Tullamore Dew
5. Redbreast

WORLD WHISKIES
1. Yamazaki 12-year-old Japanese Single Malt
2. Amrut Fusion—Indian Single Malt
3. Lark Australian Single Malt
4. Kavalan Taiwanese Single Malt
5. Millstone Dutch Rye Whisky

Resources

FESTIVALS

After the resurgence of whisky sales in the late 1980s, the whisky industry started organizing festivals to entice and educate the public. They originated in the United States and slowly spread to other countries. Festivals offer the opportunity to taste a wide selection of whiskies and attend seminars conducted by whisky experts. The following is not an exhaustive list but highlights some of the best-known festivals around the world.

AUSTRALIA

Whisky Live (Adelaide, Brisbane, Hobart, Melbourne, Perth, Sydney)

BELGIUM

International Malt Whisky Festival (Ghent)
Whisky Live (Spa)

ENGLAND

The Whisky Show (London)
Whisky Live (London)

FRANCE

Whisky Live (Paris)

GERMANY

The Whisky Fair (Limburg an der Lahn)

ISRAEL

Whisky Live (Tel Aviv)

THE NETHERLANDS

International Whisky Festival (The Hague)
Maltstock (Nijmegen)
Whisky Festival Northern Netherlands (Groningen)

POLAND

Whisky Live (Warsaw)

SCOTLAND

Feis Ile (Islay)
Spirit of Speyside Whisky Festival (Speyside)

SINGAPORE

Whisky Live

SOUTH AFRICA

Whisky Live (Capetown, Johannesburg, Pretoria)

SWEDEN

Beer and Whisky Festival (Stockholm)

UNITED STATES

Kentucky Bourbon Festival (Bardstown, Kentucky)
WhiskyFest (Chicago, Illinois; New York, New York; San Francisco, California; Washington, D.C.)
Whisky Live (Los Angeles, California; Louisville, Kentucky; New York, New York; Washington, D.C.)

ORGANIZATIONS

AMERICAN CRAFT SPIRITS ASSOCIATION

A registered nonprofit trade group representing the U.S. craft spirits industry founded in 2012. More information available at americancraftspirits.org.

AMERICAN DISTILLING INSTITUTE

U.S. trade organization for craft distillers founded in 2003. More information available at distilling.com.

DISTILLED SPIRITS COUNCIL OF THE UNITED STATES (DISCUS)

A national trade association that represents producers and marketers of distilled spirits sold in the United States, including the American whiskey industry. Founded in 1973 from the merger of three older organizations: the Bourbon Institute, the Distilled Spirits Institute, and the Licensed Beverage Industries, Inc. More information available at discus.org.

THE HONORABLE ORDER OF KENTUCKY COLONELS

An independent, nonprofit, charitable organization that recognizes individuals for noteworthy accomplishments and outstanding service to a community, state, or

nation. The title "Kentucky Colonel" was formalized in 1813, but the Honorable Order of Kentucky Colonels was established in 1932. More information available at kycolonels.org.

THE KEEPERS OF THE QUAICH

An exclusive international society that recognizes individuals who have shown outstanding commitment to the Scotch Whisky Industry, founded by the Scottish whisky industry in 1988. More information available at keepersofthequaich.co.uk.

THE SCOTCH MALT WHISKY SOCIETY (SMWS)

An international members club that purchases and bottles rare and exceptional whiskies exclusively for its members, founded in Edinburgh in 1983. More information available at smws.com.

THE SCOTCH WHISKY ASSOCIATION (SWA)

An organization that promotes, represents, and protects the interests of the Scottish whisky industry worldwide. Founded as the Wine and Spirit Brand Association in 1912, it became the SWA in 1942. More information available at scotch-whisky.org.uk.

READING

BOOKS

Arthur, Helen. *The Single Malt Whisky Companion*. Hoboken: John Wiley & Sons, 1997.
———. *A Teacher's Tale: 175 Years of Scotch Whisky Through the Eyes of William Teacher & Sons*. Bristol, UK: Allied Domecq Spirits and Wine, 2005.

———. *Whisky: The Water of Life—Uisge Beatha*. Richmond Hill, ON: Firefly Books, 2000.
Barnard, Alfred. *The Whisky Distilleries of the United Kingdom*. New York: Harper's Weekly Gazette, 1887.
Behr, Edward. *Prohibition: Thirteen Years That Changed America*. New York: Arcade, 1996.

Bell, Darek. *Alt Whiskeys: Alternative Whiskeys and Techniques for the Adventurous Craft Distiller*. Nashville: Corsair Artisan Distillery, 2012.

———. *Fire Water: Experimental Smoked Malts and Whiskeys*. Nashville: Corsair Artisan Distillery, 2014.

Broom, Dave. *The World Atlas of Whisky: New Edition*. London: Mitchell Beazley, 2014.

Bruce-Gardyne, Tom. *The Scotch Whisky Book*. Edinburgh: Lomond Books, 2002.

Bruce Lockhart, Sir Robert. *Scotch: The Whisky of Scotland in Fact and Story*. London: Putnam, 1951.

Bryson, Lew. *Tasting Whiskey: An Insider's Guide to the Unique Pleasures of the World's Finest Spirits*. North Adams, MA: Storey, 2014.

Buxrud, Ulf. *Japanese Whisky: Facts, Figures and Taste*. Limhamn, Swed.: DataAnalys Scandinavia, 2007.

Buxton, Ian. *101 Whiskies to Try Before You Die*. London: Headline, 2010.

Buxton, Ian, and Paul S. Hughes. *The Science and Commerce of Whisky*. London: Royal Society of Chemistry, 2013.

Carson, Gerald. *The Social History of Bourbon*. Lexington: University Press of Kentucky, 2010.

Cecil, Sam K. *Bourbon: The Evolution of Kentucky Whiskey*. Nashville: Turner, 2010.

———. *The Evolution of the Bourbon Whiskey Industry in Kentucky*. Nashville: Turner, 2001.

Cowdery, Charles K. *Bourbon, Straight: The Uncut and Unfiltered Story of American Whiskey*. Chicago: Made and Bottled in Kentucky, 2004.

———. *Bourbon, Strange: Surprising Stories on American Whiskey*. Chicago: Made and Bottled in Kentucky, 2014.

Daiches, David. *Scotch Whisky: Its Past and Present*. London: André Deutsch, 1969.

Darwen, James. *The Illustrated History of Whisky*. Suffolk, UK: Harold Starke, 1993.

Getz, Oscar. *Whiskey: An American Pictorial History*. Philadelphia: David McKay, 1978.

Givens, Ron. *Bourbon at Its Best: The Lore and Allure of America's Finest Spirits*. Cincinnati: Clerisy Press, 2008.

Green, Ben A. *Jack Daniel's Legacy*. Lynchburg, VA: Rich Printing, 1967.

Greenberg, Emanuel and Madeline. *Whiskey in the Kitchen: The Lively Art of Cooking with Bourbon, Scotch, Rum, Brandy, Gin, Liqueurs, and Kindred Spirits*. New York: Bobbs-Merrill, 1968.

Greene, Heather. *Whiskey Distilled: A Populist Guide to the Water of Life*. New York: Avery, 2014.

Grindal, Richard. *Return to the Glen*. Chevy Chase, MD: Alvin Rosenbaum Projects, 1989.

Gunn, Neil M. *Whisky and Scotland*. London: George Routledge & Sons, 1935.

Hills, Phillip. *Appreciating Whisky: The Connoisseur's Guide to Nosing, Tasting, and Enjoying Scotch*. New York: HarperCollins, 2000.

Hopkins, Kate. *99 Drams of Whiskey: The Accidental Hedonist's Quest for the Perfect Shot and the History of the Drink*. New York: St. Martin's Press, 2009.

Huckelbridge, Dane. *Bourbon: A History of the American Spirit*. New York: William Morrow, 2014.

Jackson, Michael. *Malt Whisky Companion*, 6th ed. London: DK, 2010.

———. *Whiskey: The Definitive World Guide*. London: DK, 2005.

Kane, Frank. *Anatomy of the Whisky Business*. Manhasset, NY: Lakehouse Press, 1965.

Kergommeaux, Davin de. *Canadian Whisky: The Portable Expert.* Toronto: McClelland & Stewart, 2012.

Krass, Peter. *Blood & Whiskey: The Life and Times of Jack Daniel.* Hoboken: John Wiley & Sons, 2004.

MacDonald, Aeneas. *Whisky.* Edinburgh: Porpoise Press, 1930.

Macilwain, Ian. *Bottled History.* London: Envisage Books, 2007.

MacKenzie, Compton. *Whisky Galore.* London: Penguin, 1957.

MacLean, Charles. *Famous for a Reason: The Story of The Famous Grouse.* Edinburgh: Birlinn, 2015.

———. *MacLean's Miscellany of Whisky.* London: Little Books, 2010.

———. *Malt Whisky.* London: Mitchell Beazley, 1997.

———. *Scotch Whisky: A Liquid History.* London: Cassell Illustrated, 2004.

———. *Spirit of Place: Scotland's Great Whisky Distilleries.* London: Frances Lincoln, 2015.

———. *World Whisky.* London: DK, 2009.

McDowell, R. J. S. *Whiskies of Scotland.* London: John Murray, 1967.

Milroy, Wallace. *The Original Malt Whisky Almanac: A Taster's Guide,* 7th ed. Castle Douglas, UK: Neil Wilson, 1998.

Milsted, David, *The Bluffer's Guide to Whisky.* London: Oval Books, 2005.

Minnick, Fred. *Women & Whiskey: The Untold Story of How Women Saved Bourbon, Scotch, and Irish Whiskey.* Lincoln, NE: Potomac Books, 2013.

Mitenbuler, Reid. *Bourbon Empire: The Past and Future of America's Whiskey.* New York: Viking, 2015.

Morrice, Philip. *Schweppes Guide to Scotch.* Dorset, UK: Alpha Books, 1983.

Moss, Michael, and John R. Hume. *The Making of Scotch Whisky: A History of the Scotch Whisky Distilling Industry.* London: James & James, 1981.

Mulryan, Peter. *The Whiskeys of Ireland.* Dublin: O'Brien Press, 2002.

Murray, Jim. *The Art of Whisky: A Deluxe Blend of Historic Posters from the Public Record Office.* Surrey, UK: PRO Publications, 1998.

———. *Classic Blended Scotch.* London: Prion Books, 1999.

———. *Classic Bourbon, Tennessee & Rye Whiskey.* London: Prion Books, 1998.

———. *Classic Irish Whiskey.* London: Prion Books, 1997.

———. *Jim Murray's Complete Book of Whisky.* London: Carlton Books, 1997.

———. *Jim Murray's Whisky Bible.* Atlanta: Whitman Publishing, LLC, 2015.

Nettleton, J. A. *The Manufacture of Whisky and Plain Spirit.* Aberdeen, UK: G. Cornwall & Sons, 1913.

Nouet, Martine. *À Table: Whisky from Glass to Plate.* Isle of Islay, UK: Ailsa Press, 2016.

O'Connor, Fionnán. *A Glass Apart: Irish Single Pot Still Whiskey.* Victoria, Austral.: Images, 2015.

Okrent, Daniel. *Last Call: The Rise and Fall of Prohibition.* New York: Scribner, 2011.

Pacult, F. Paul. *American Still Life: The Jim Beam Story and the Making of the World's #1 Bourbon.* Hoboken: John Wiley & Sons, 2003.

———. *A Double Scotch: How Chivas Regal and The Glenlivet Became Global Icons.* Hoboken: John Wiley & Sons, 2005.

Paterson, Richard, and Gavin D. Smith. *Goodness Nose: The Passionate Revelations of a Scotch Whisky Master Blender.* Castle Douglas, UK: Neil Wilson, 2008.

Rannie, William F. *Canadian Whisky: The Product and the Industry.* Beamsville, ON: W. F. Rannie, 1976.

Regan, Gary, and Mardee Haidin Regan. *The Book of Bourbon: And Other Fine American Whiskeys.* New York: Houghton Mifflin, 1995.

Ridley, Neil, and Gavin D. Smith. *Let Me Tell You About Whisky: Taste, Try, and Enjoy Whisky from Around the World*. London: Pavilion, 2014.

Ridley, Neil, and Joel Harrison. *Distilled: From Absinthe and Brandy to Vodka and Whisky, the World's Finest Artisan Spirits Unearthed, Explained, and Enjoyed*. London: Mitchell Beazley, 2015.

Risen, Clay. *American Whiskey, Bourbon & Rye: A Guide to the Nation's Favorite Spirit*. New York: Sterling Epicure, 2013.

Rogers, Adam. *Proof: The Science of Booze*. New York: Mariner Books, 2015

Ronde, Ingvar. *Malt Whisky Yearbook 2016*. Shrewsbury, UK: MagDig Media, 2015.

Roskrow, Dominic. *Whisky Japan: The Essential Guide to the World's Most Exotic Whisky*. New York: Kodansha USA, 2016.

———. *1001 Whiskies You Must Taste Before You Die*. New York: Universe, 2012.

Roskrow, Dominic, and Gavin D. Smith. *Whiskey Opus*. London: DK, 2012.

Ross, James. *Whisky*. London: Routledge & Kegan Paul, 1970.

Rothbaum, Noah. *The Art of American Whiskey: A Visual History of the Nation's Most Storied Spirit, Through 100 Iconic Labels*. Berkeley: Ten Speed Press, 2015.

Russell, Inge, and Graham Stewart. *Whisky—Technology, Production and Marketing*, 2nd ed. London: Elsevier, 2014.

Saintsbury, George. *Notes on a Cellar-Book*. London: MacMillan, 1920.

Samuels, Bill Jr. *Maker's Mark: My Autobiography*. Louisville: Saber, 2000.

Scott, Berkeley and Jeanine. *The Kentucky Bourbon Trail*. Charleston, SC: Arcadia, 2009.

Skipworth, Mark. *The Scotch Whisky Book*. London: Lomond Books, 1992.

Steadman, Ralph. *Still Life with Bottle: Whisky According to Ralph Steadman*. London: Random House, 1994.

Stephenson, Tristan. *The Curious Bartender: An Odyssey of Malt, Bourbon & Rye Whiskies*. New York: Ryland Peters & Small, 2014.

Taylor, Richard. *The Great Crossing: A Historic Journey to Buffalo Trace Distillery*. Frankfort, KY: Buffalo Trace Distillery, 2002.

Townsend, Brian. *Scotch Missed: The Original Guide to the Lost Distilleries of Scotland*. Castle Douglas, UK: Angels' Share, 2015. First published in 1993.

Truths About Whisky. Dublin: Jameson, Power & Roe, 1878.

Van Winkle Campbell, Sally. *But Always Fine Bourbon: Pappy van Winkle and the Story of Old Fitzgerald*. Louisville: Limestone Lane Press, 1999.

Veach, Michael R. *Kentucky Bourbon Whiskey: An American Heritage*. Lexington: University Press of Kentucky, 2013.

Warth, Ralph L. *Liquid Gold: Investing Successfully in Whisky*. New York: Windsor Verlag, 2014.

Watman, Max. *Chasing the White Dog: An Amateur Outlaw's Adventures in Moonshine*. New York: Simon & Schuster, 2010.

Wilson, Neil. *The Island Whisky Trail*. Castle Douglas, UK: Angels' Share, 2003.

———. *Scotch and Water*. Isle of Colonsay, UK: Lochar, 1985.

Wilson, Ross. *Scotch Made Easy*. London: Hutchinson, 1959.

Wishart, David. *Whisky Classified: Choosing Single Malts by Flavour*, 3rd ed. London: Pavilion Books, 2012.

Young, Al. *Four Roses—The Return of a Whiskey Legend*. Louisville: Butler Books, 2011.

ALSO BY THIS AUTHOR

Offringa, Hans. *A Taste of Whisky*. Zwolle, Neth.: Conceptual Continuity, 2007.

———. *Whisky & Jazz*. Charleston, SC: EPPC, 2009.

———. *Bourbon & Blues*. Charleston, SC: Conceptual Continuity, 2011.

———. *Malts & Jazz*. Charleston, SC: Conceptual Continuity, 2012.

———. *Rum & Reggae*. Charleston, SC: Conceptual Continuity, 2013.

———. *Still Stories: Whisky Tales from Kentucky to Kilbeggan*. Charleston, SC: Conceptual Continuity, 2016.

Offringa, Hans, Mark Lawson, and John LaDell. *The Craigellachie Collection of Scotch Whisky Labels*. Parts 1 & 2. Elgin, UK: Gopher, 1998-99.

Offringa, Hans, and Marcel van Gils. *1815–2015: 200 Years of Laphroaig*. Zwolle, Neth.: Conceptual Continuity, 2015.

MAGAZINES

Whiskeria
Whisky Advocate (United States)
Whisky Magazine (United Kingdom)
Whisky Quarterly

TRAVEL

In the context of this book it is impossible to publish a comprehensive list of all whisky bars in the United States and worldwide. What follows is a selection of favorite places suggested by whisky aficionados from all over the world.

WHISK(E)Y BARS

UNITED STATES

Atlanta, Georgia
Whisky Mistress, 3161 Maple Drive NE

Austin, Texas
The Blackheart, 86 Rainey Street

Bardstown, Kentucky
Old Talbott Tavern, 107 W. Stephen Foster Avenue

Boston, Massachusetts
The Last Hurrah, 60 School Street

Boulder, Colorado
The West End Tavern, 926 Pearl Street

Brooklyn, New York
Noorman's Kil, 609 Grand Street

Charleston, South Carolina
Blind Tiger Pub, 36–38 Broad Street
The Gin Joint, 182 E. Bay Street
Husk, 76 Queen Street
Prohibition, 547 King Street
Seanachai, 3157 Maybank Highway, John's Island

Chicago, Illinois
Delilah's Chicago, 2771 N. Lincoln Avenue

Dallas, Texas
Trinity Hall, 5321 E. Mockingbird Lane,
#250

Denver, Colorado
Pints Pub, 221 W. 13th Avenue

Houston, Texas
Anvil Bar & Refuge, 1424 Westheimer
Road
Poison Girl, 1641 Westheimer Road,
Suite B

Indianapolis, Indiana
MacNiven's, 339 Massachusetts Avenue

Las Vegas, Nevada
Double Helix Wine & Whiskey Lounge,
6599 Las Vegas Boulevard S., #150B
Oak & Ivy, Downtown Container Park,
707 Fremont Street

Los Angeles, California
Seven Grand, 515 W. 7th Street

Louisville, Kentucky
Bourbons Bistro, 2255 Frankfort Avenue
Old Seelbach Bar, 500 S. 4th Street

Memphis, Tennessee
Alchemy Memphis, 940 S. Cooper Street

Miami, Florida
Taurus Beer & Whisk(e)y House,
3540 Main Highway C103

Minneapolis, Minnesota
Butcher & the Boar, 1121 Hennepin
Avenue

Nashville, Tennessee
Whiskey Kitchen, 118 12th Avenue S.

New Haven, Connecticut
The Owl Shop, 268 College Street

New Orleans, Louisiana
Barrel Proof, 1201 Magazine Street

New York, New York
Brandy Library, 25 N. Moore Street
The Flatiron Room, 37 W. 26th Street
Highlands, 150 W. 10th Street

Philadelphia, Pennsylvania
Monk's Cafe, 264 S. 16th Street

Portland, Oregon
Multnomah Whisky Library,
1124 SW Alder Street

Raleigh, North Carolina
Whiskey Kitchen, 201 W. Martin Street

St. Louis, Missouri
The Scottish Arms, 8 S. Sarah Street

San Diego, California
The Whiskey House, 420 3rd Avenue

San Francisco, California
Nihon Whisky Lounge, 1779 Folsom
Street

Santa Monica, California
The Daily Pint, 2310 Pico Boulevard

Seattle, Washington
Bourbon & Bones, 4350 Leary Way NW
Canon, 928 12th Avenue
The Pike Pub and Brewery, 1415 1st
Avenue
The Whisky Bar, 2122 2nd Avenue

Washington, D.C.
Jack Rose Dining Saloon, 2007 18th
Street NW

WORLDWIDE

Australia
The Baxter Inn, 152-156 Clarence Street, Sydney
Boilermaker House, 209-211 Lonsdale Street, Melbourne
Helvetica, Rear 101 St Georges Terrace, Perth
Whisky & Alement, 270 Russell Street, Melbourne

Belgium
De Cluysenaer, Kluizendorpstraat 82, Kluizen
The Glengarry, Sint-Baafsplein 32, Ghent
The Green Man, Koningsstraat 64, Oostende

Canada
The Dam Pub, 53 Bruce Street, Thornbury, ON
The Feathers Pub, 962 Kingston Road, Toronto, ON
Fets Whisky Kitchen, 1230 Commercial Drive, Vancouver, BC
Shebeen Whiskey House, 212 Carrall Street, Vancouver, BC

Czech Republic
Whiskeria Bar, Jindřišská Věž, Prague

Denmark
Kruts Karport, Øster Farimagsgade 12, Copenhagen
Lidkoeb, Vesterbrogade 72B, Copenhagen
Torvehallerne, Fiskergade 2-8, Vejle

England
Black Rock, 9 Christopher Street, London
Blues Kitchen, 111-113 Camden High Street, 134-146 Curtain Road, and 40 Acre Lane, London
Boisdale of Canary Wharf, Cabot Place, Canary Wharf, London

France
Harry's New York Bar, 5 Rue Daunou, Paris
Wallace Bar, 2 Rue Octavio Mey, Lyon

Germany
Brachmanns Galeron, Hein-Hoyer-Strasse 60, Hamburg
Loch Ness Scottish Pub and Whisky Bar, Roonstrasse 31A, Berlin
Offside Pub & Whisky Bar, Jülicher Strasse 4, Berlin
Ryan's Muddy Boot, Schlörstrasse 10, Munich
Villa Konthor, Werner-Senger-Strasse 23, Limburg an der Lahn
Whisky Spirits, Wallstrasse 23, Frankfurt

Ireland
Beaufort Bar & Restaurant, Beaufort, Killarney
Cronin's Pub, 1 Point Road, Crosshaven
Fairhill House Hotel, An Fhairce, Clonbur
The Galtee Inn, The Square, Cahir
Garavan's, 46 William Street, Galway
Lowry's Bar, Market Street, Clifden
O'Loclainn's Irish Whiskey Bar, Ballyvaughn
The Palace Bar, 21 Fleet Street, Dublin
South County Bar, Douglas Village, Douglas, Cork

Israel
The Bear Pub, Hanassi Avenue 135, Haifa

Japan
Bar Augusta, Arakawa Building 1F, 2-3 Tsurunocho, Kita-ku, Osaka
Highlander Inn, one-minute walk from Nakanosakaue Metro Station, Tokyo
Mash Tun, 2-14-3 Kamiosaki Shinagawa, Tokyo

Wodka Tonic (Don't be fooled by the name; it's a fine whisky bar!) Tamura Building B1F, 2 Chome 25-11 Nishi Azabu, Minato-ku, Tokyo

Lithuania
King and Mouse, Vilnius

Malaysia
The Whisky Bar, 46 Changkat Bukit Bintang, Bukit Bintang, Kuala Lumpur

The Netherlands
Door 74, Reguliersdwarsstraat 74I, Amsterdam

The Hielander, Ridderstraat 15, Alkmaar

Jack's Music Bar, Sassenstraat 29, Zwolle

J.D. William's Whisky Bar, Prinsenstraat 5, Amsterdam

Whiskycafe L&B, Korte Leidsedwarsstraat 82-84, Amsterdam

Northern Ireland
Bittles Bar, Musgrave Channel Road, Belfast

The Duke of York, 7-11 Commercial Court, Belfast

McCuaig's Bar, Ballycastle, Rathlin Island

Norway
Dr. Jekyll's Pub, Klingenberggata 4, Oslo

Poland
Dom Whisky, Droga Rybacka 60, Jastrzębia Góra

Russia
Grand Bourbon Street, 2 Potapovskiy Lane, Moscow

Whisky Bar, Nekrasova Street 9, St. Petersburg

Scotland
Bon Accord, 153 North Street, Glasgow

Copper Dog, Craigellachie Hotel, Victoria Street, Craigellachie

The Devil's Advocate, 9 Advocates Close, Edinburgh

Dornoch Castle Hotel, Castle Street, Dornoch

Fiddler's, The Village Green, Drumnadrochit

Gleneagles, Auchterarder

The Highlander Inn, Victoria Street, Craigellachie

The Jazz Bar, 1A Chambers Street, Edinburgh

The Mash Tun, Broomfield Square, Aberlour

The Pot Still, 154 Hope Street, Glasgow

The Quaich, Craigellachie Hotel, Victoria Street, Craigellachie

Scotch Malt Whisky Society (SMWS), 28 Queen Street (Bar & Restaurant) and 87 Giles Street (Members Club), Edinburgh

Tannochbrae, 22 Fife Street, Dufftown

Whiski Rooms, 4-7 North Bank Street, Edinburgh

Singapore
The Auld Alliance, Rendezvous Hotel, 9 Bras Basah Road, Singapore

South Africa
Wild about Whisky, Auldstone House, 506 Naledi Drive, Dullstroom

Spain
Bar de Copas Whiskey, Calle Alcalde Sainz de Baranda 51, Madrid

Sweden
Akkurat Bar & Restaurant, Hornsgatan 18, Stockholm

Ardbeg Embassy, Västerlånggatan 68, Stockholm

The Bishop's Arms, Kungsportsavenyn 36, Goteborg

The Bishops Arms, Gustav Adolfs Torg 49C, Malmö

Saddle & Sabre Saloon & Steakhouse, Tegnérgatan 9, Stockholm

Switzerland

Smallest Whisky Bar on Earth, Platz 71, Santa Maria Val Müstair

Widder Bar, Widdergasse 6, Zürich

Taiwan

L'arrière-cour, Xinyi Ahnhe Station Exit 2, Taipei

WHISKY HOTELS

Scotland is the only country with dedicated whisky hotels, so the following list is Scotland-centric.

Craigellachie Hotel, Victoria Street, Speyside, Banffshire AB38 9SR, UK

Dornoch Castle Hotel, Castle Street, Dornoch, Sutherland IV25 3SD, UK

Highlander Inn, Victoria Street, Craigellachie, Banffshire AB38 9SR, UK

Fiddler's, The Village Green, Drumnadrochit, Inverness, Inverness-shire IV63 6TX, UK

The Torridon, Achnasheen, Wester Ross IV22 2EY, UK

WHISKY TRAILS

American Whiskey Trail (United States), americanwhiskeytrail.com

Ireland Whiskey Trail (Ireland), irelandwhiskeytrail.com

Kentucky Bourbon Trail (United States), kybourbontrail.com

Malt Whisky Trail (Scotland), maltwhiskytrail.com

WHISKY TRAVEL AGENCIES

A non-exhaustive list of travel agencies that organize specialized whisky tours:

European Waterways (gobarging.com)

Jewish Travel Agency (jewishtravelagency.com)

Lynott Tours, Inc. (lynotttours.com)

McLean Scotland (mcleanscotland.com)

Scotland Sailing (scotlandsailing.com)

Speyside Whisky Experience (speysidewhiskyexperience.com)

Thalassa (tallshipthalassa.nl/en)

The Travel Club (thetravelclub.nl/info/to-our-english-visitors)

Acknowledgments

The author would like to thank the following people and institutions: Charlie, my dear friend, for letting me use his Tasting Wheel; my beloved Lady Jane Waring and my American brother Charles W. Waring III for continuous moral support, a wonderful place to write, and lots of inspiration; Mr. Calhoun "Callie" Witham Jr., for being an excellent roommate, joining me in emptying the odd bottle of whisky, and inspiring the term *callied;* the Craigellachie Hotel, Ron Greve, Kevin Kroon, Ewald Lap, and Teun van Wel for additional photography; Ingvar Ronde for figures; Fred Feenstra, Matthijs Hakfoort, Sietse Offringa, Robbert Sas, and Ronald Zwartepoorte for reading the original manuscript and for their excellent feedback; Willemien Haagsma, Francis Wehkamp, Sofie Langenberg, and Chris de Graaf at Karakter Uitgevers; Judy Pray, Mura Dominko, Sibylle Kazeroid, and Renata Di Biase at Artisan; designers Erik Marinovich and Raphael Geroni; the many whisky lovers worldwide who flooded me with suggestions and questions—simply too many to mention individually, hence a collective big thank-you to all. Without the help of all these people I would not have been able to make a book like this. Last but not least, my wife and muse, and the female half of the Whisky Couple, Becky Lovett Offringa.

Index

HANS OFFRINGA is an internationally renowned author and whisky expert, recognized as Keeper of the Quaich, Honorary Scotsman, Patron of the Whisky Festival in Northern Netherlands, and Kentucky Colonel, among other honors. He is also the contributing editor for Europe for *Whisky Magazine;* a lecturer at the International Whisky School in Groningen, Netherlands; and, with his wife Becky Lovett Offringa, a judge at the Dutch Whisky Awards.

"MY OWN EXPERIENCE HAS BEEN THAT THE TOOLS I NEED FOR MY TRADE ARE PAPER, TOBACCO, FOOD, AND A LITTLE WHISKY."

William Faulkner